LABRANG

A TIBETAN BUDDHIST MONASTERY
AT THE CROSSROADS OF FOUR CIVILIZATIONS

LABRANG

A TIBETAN BUDDHIST MONASTERY
AT THE CROSSROADS OF FOUR CIVILIZATIONS

by
Paul Kocot Nietupski

Photos from
The Griebenow Archives, 1921-1949

Snow Lion Publications
Ithaca, New York

Snow Lion Publications
P.O. Box 6483
Ithaca, New York 14851 USA
607-273-8519

ISBN 1-55939-090-5

Printed in Canada

Library of Congress Cataloging-in-Publication Data
Nietupski, Paul Kocot, 1950-
        Labrang : a Tibetan Buddhist monastery at the crossroads of four
    civilizations / by Paul Kocot Nietupski. -- 1st ed.
            p.   cm.
        Includes bibliographical references.
        ISBN 1-55939-090-5
        1. Labrang (Monastery : Tibet)   2. A-mdo (China) -- Civilization.
    I. Title.
    BQ6349.L34N54   1998
    294.3'657'09515--dc21   98-5347
                                                                      CIP

TABLE OF CONTENTS

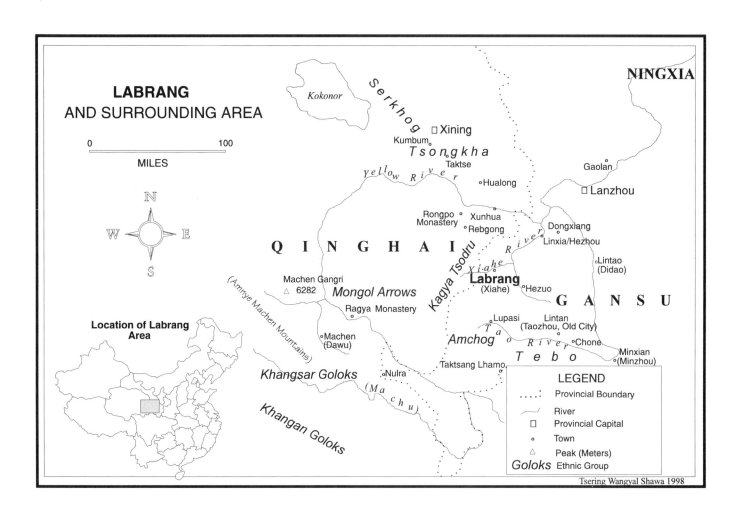

LABRANG
AND SURROUNDING AREA

0 ————————— 100
MILES

N
W · E
S

Location of Labrang Area

NINGXIA

Kokonor

Serkhog

□ Xining
Kumbum

Tsongkha

Taktse

Yellow River

Gaolan

□ Lanzhou

Hualong

Rongpo Monastery
Xunhua
Rebgong

Dongxiang

Linxia/Hezhou

Kagya Tsodru

Xiahe

River

Lintao (Didao)

Q I N G H A I

Machen Gangri
△ 6282

Mongol Arrows

Labrang
(Xiahe)

Hezuo

G A N S U

Ragya Monastery

Machen (Dawu)

(Amnye Machen Mountains)

Lupasi

Lintan (Taozhou, Old City)

Amchog

Tao River

Chone

Minxian (Minzhou)

Tebo

Khangsar Goloks

Nulra

Taktsang Lhamo

(Machu)

Khangan Goloks

LEGEND
·······	Provincial Boundary
⌇	River
□	Provincial Capital
○	Town
△	Peak (Meters)
Goloks	Ethnic Group

Tsering Wangyal Shawa 1998

PREFACE AND ACKNOWLEDGMENTS

This small book is the result of several years of research and the cooperation of several individuals and institutions. In 1989, Mei Griebenow, then the holder of the Griebenow photographs, initiated a project to preserve and document her family's experience of Tibet and the unique culture her grandparents encountered at Labrang and in Amdo. The Griebenow family donated their entire collection of photographs to Tibet House, New York, whose staff in turn provided Snow Lion Publications with a sample of the photographs for this book. What at first appeared to be a fairly simple task of identifying the photographs gradually grew in complexity, far beyond the limits of this volume.

I began by studying and identifying the entire Griebenow photographic and written collections and collecting and surveying the massive and still growing range of supplementary materials in Tibetan, Chinese, and English. I interviewed as many of the persons who lived in or visited Labrang during the Griebenow mission years (1922-1949), including persons now living in the United States, India, and Gansu Province PRC, and collected as much written first-hand testimony as I could find. Much more information came to light than I had originally anticipated.

For help received, many thanks especially to Wendy and Val Nietupski, to the late Pema Losang Chogyen, and to Bob and Nena Thurman, Tsering Wangyal Shawa (cartography), Christopher Atwood, Charlene Makley, Peter F. Skinner, Mel Goldstein, Elliot Sperling, Beata Tikos, Wolfgang von Erffa, Pam Mason, Matt Berg, Joseph Wenninger, Nita Fowler, Sidney Piburn, Susan Kyser, Jesse Townsley, and to the Graduate Research Committee of John Carroll University. Thanks are also due to the Alo family, Prof. Jigme Norbu (Alak Taktser), Losang Tenzin, Tashi Tsering, Lhamo Tsering, Jigme Lhundrup, Narkyid Nawang Dondrup, and Alak Tsayi (Tenzin Palbar). Finally, His Holiness the Dalai Lama, himself from a village in Amdo not far from Labrang, provided much assistance and encouragement.

Any attempt to present a massive amount of data in a short format recalls the tip of an iceberg maxim; much remains hidden. Necessarily, work on this project continues. This volume presents a small amount of data representative of a much larger whole. Any errors in the narrative, structure, and identifications throughout are mine.

Paul Nietupski
John Carroll University
Cleveland
February 1998

Technical Note

Many place names important to this story have changed since 1949; many of the persons involved have several different names. I have chosen to render Tibetan and Mongol names in approximate English phonetic equivalents, to use Chinese names for the Muslims (as the Hui and Turkic-speaking Salars themselves usually do), and to use the Chinese Pinyin system for Chinese names, except when a Wade-Giles or other spelling system is better known to English readers, as in the case of Chiang Kai-shek, for example, whose name in Pinyin is Jiang Jieshi. Additionally, I have attempted to use the modern names of places, but preserve the old names when quoting primary sources. Further, when discussing a distinctively Tibetan region or person, I generally use a Tibetan name, and when discussing a Chinese region or person, a Chinese name. When a border region or person was popularly known by both Chinese and Tibetan names, I note this and choose one. Further, for ease of understanding, I refer to Gonpo Dondrup's entire extended clan as the "Alo" family, though all members had their own personal name(s) and/or titles and also Chinese names, all of which I note. I also attempt to include the Chinese names of those Tibetans who played important roles in negotiations and alliances with the Chinese, since even though Tibetan, in Chinese sources they are most often referred to only by their Chinese names. Throughout the text I follow the convention of many primary sources and often refer to Labrang Monastery, the properties it owned and the territories it controlled with the single word "Labrang."

INTRODUCTION

The materials I used for this book barely scrape the surface of the growing resources on Labrang and Amdo, located in modern-day southern Gansu Province, People's Republic of China. The primary sources of information are the Griebenow Archive photographs,[1] written and oral memoirs of the Griebenow and Alo families, interviews, and selected secondary sources in Tibetan, Chinese, and English.

The photographic and written records of the Griebenow family document their experiences at Labrang and their work as Christian missionaries from 1922 to 1949. It is fortunate that Marion Griebenow took about three thousand photographs, and that he and Blanche, his wife, wrote about their experiences so consistently over the years of their stay. The Griebenows' work and adventures themselves illustrate what twentieth-century life at Labrang was like. These photographic and written windows into Labrang Monastery and its territories offer clear pictures of the people and their cultures.

The Griebenows were Christian missionaries who came to Labrang to spread the message of the Christian Gospels. Their writing, like that of many missionaries, is predictably evangelical and occasionally condescending. I have done my best to select some of their most descriptive and insightful passages about Labrang for inclusion here. It is noteworthy that the Griebenows did not keep distant from their hosts; they were known for their depth of understanding of the Tibetans, their fluency in the Tibetan language, and their willingness to personally engage the Tibetans on religious subjects. Their proximity to the Tibetans gives their records a credibility not often found in missionaries' accounts.

One of the most frequent subjects in the Griebenow photographic and written materials is the extended Tibetan clan who rose to power at Labrang during their stay. I have chosen to refer to the entire clan with a single name, Alo, even though this oversimplifies their own diversity. Further, my focus on this extended family is not intended to assert that these people were self-sacrificing civil servants. The focus on the Alos aims to show their actual status at Labrang from the perspectives of the Tibetan population-at-large and the larger picture of regional power struggles. Like other important clans in Amdo, they were members of a Tibetan ruling elite in an ethnic borderland. They probably felt that their best interests also served those of the Labrang community, a sentiment not necessarily shared by every single Labrang Tibetan. Still, they were the prominent family in the region, with two reincarnate Buddhist leaders in their midst, which gave them credibility in the eyes of much of the community.

The history and politics of Labrang's predominantly Muslim neighbors to the north and northwest are long and complex subjects. Since this is a short book on Labrang Monastery and its territories I often refer to these neighbors collectively as "Hui" (except when quoting contemporary English-language documents), even though this usage reduces the diversity of the Salars, the Dongxiang and the Hui to a generic term. Further, I sometimes use "Hui" to refer to the Muslim Qinghai forces, to the Ninghai Army, to troops and people under the leadership of the extended Ma family, and to Gansu ethnic groups[2] near Labrang.[3] When I do use the term "Muslim" I am not referring to the teachings and practices of Islam, unless so specified. I use this word only as a broad descriptive term for the distinctive Chinese Muslim culture, because the Gansu- and Qinghai-based fighters and political leaders were not acting in the name of Islam.[4]

The issues raised in this book become even more complicated after a closer look at Chinese politics during the early twentieth century. This was the pre-Communist Republican, or "warlord" period (1911-1949), which was an especially crucial and unstable period in Asian history. The instability of the times played an important role in the events that took place at Labrang Monastery. Even though both the Chinese and the Muslims claimed sovereignty over Labrang and the Alos, their claims were only nominal. For example, before 1927 the Chinese and Muslims regarded Labrang as part of Qinghai, with little regard to Labrang's subject territories. In 1927 the Chinese negotiated a treaty with the Qinghai government that moved the borderline so that Labrang was located in Gansu. The point here is that the Chinese government had little real control over the Qinghai forces and over the Labrang Tibetans. At Labrang, as in other territories throughout this Sino-Tibetan border region, political and legal control were the result of each place's history of relations with its neighbors.

The monastery itself has a long and convoluted history of growth and development, with a complex web of events, persons, cultures, and national groups that helped shape it

into the form witnessed by the Griebenows. It is located in a unique place, near a major trade route that links East and Central Asia, and borders four Asian civilizations—Tibetan, Mongol, Muslim and Chinese. Labrang's position on the borders of the Mongol, Muslim, Chinese and Tibetan ethnic nations and its proximity to trade routes contributed to the development of a volatile atmosphere.[5]

If this were not enough, the fact that Labrang was one of the largest Tibetan Buddhist monasteries that has ever existed, with the full panoply of Tibetan academic and ritual programs operating on a grand scale, in an ethnically diverse setting, makes any concise presentation difficult. This book relies on portions of several accounts of the Labrang region with photographic corroboration to document the livelihoods of the people, the government, the religion and economy at Labrang and in its subject territories.

Religion for both the Tibetan Buddhists and their non-Buddhist neighbors was of pivotal importance in everyday life. While it is incorrect to label these ethnic Tibetans as orthodox Buddhists with knowledge of philosophy and ethical practices, it is also an oversight to ignore the Tibetans' belief systems. Their beliefs helped them cope with Labrang's harsh environment, with misfortune, calamity, disease, and death. It helped in decision-making on even the most mundane levels. When to plant, to harvest, to go to market, whether or not to buy new animals, and so on were all matters about which the Labrang Tibetans consulted their religious counsellors. These questions were of vital importance to the early twentieth-century people of the Labrang region. Divinities, demons, the forces of good and evil, and the ultimate were very real to these people, and anyone who hoped for success was well advised to ascertain the status of his endeavor with respect to the unseen forces of religion. The lamas and prognosticators of Labrang were well equipped to provide advice. As elsewhere, even in the so-called secular West, religion played an important and primary role in people's lives. "One can see the force of faith in religion; Labrang Monastery enjoyed great power and prestige in Amdo."[6]

At Labrang, Tibetan Buddhism, with the Gelukpa system as a foundation, touched the lives of most twentieth-century Tibetans. "Tibetan Buddhism" here means the whole range of religious practices followed by the Tibetans that gave options for behavior that the common Tibetan could understand as being *for me, for us.*"[7] That is, Buddhism told the Tibetans "what knowledge/understanding is *worth having,*"[8] and what knowledge or understanding would result in successful and happy outcomes for individuals and the community. Religious experts tell the communities-at-large what has meaning in life and in the after- or lack-of-afterlife. This is "public theology,"[9] and it is a force that moved Tibetans to act with conviction, pride, and self-consciousness as Tibetans. The Griebenows came face-to-face with these beliefs and the full repertoire of Tibetan Buddhist ritual practices.

Another important peculiarity at Labrang found in few other Tibetan border areas was the system of the "unity of religious and political authority" in the hands of the grand incarnate Lama at Labrang. The highest political authority and the highest religious authority in the early twentieth century were in the hands of the lineage of Jamyang Shaypas.[10] This lineage considered itself at least nominally subject to the religious authority of the Dalai Lamas in central Tibet. As Joseph Fletcher has written, "[r]eligious affiliations had political significance and it should be remembered that religion in Tibetan eyes was not clearly distinguishable from political allegiances."[11] This created a sense of Labrang as a power center in Amdo with endorsements and blessings from the central Tibetans. Since Labrang Monastery was historically related to the Kadampa and Gelukpa Tibetan Buddhist orders of central Tibet, and since the lineage of Jamyang Shaypas has a close connection with the major central Tibetan monasteries, Labrang Monastery maintained a close relationship with the government and authority of the Dalai Lamas. Again in Fletcher's words, the relationship between the Dalai Lamas and Labrang "was through religious affiliation that had underlying political significance, as with the local chiefs of Amdo and eastern Kham."[12]

To demonstrate and affirm this relationship, in 1937 Labrang sent a delegation to Lhasa for an extended stay. The group included the Fifth Jamyang Shaypa, his family and a large retinue of escorts and bodyguards. While in Lhasa they met with representatives from Reting (*Rva sgreng*), Drepung (*'Bras spungs*), and several other major central Tibetan monasteries and seats of power, reaffirming Labrang's solidarity with the central tradition.[13] Although this allegiance was very real, it should be remembered that the small Tibetan kingdoms and ethnic groups in the Labrang region struggled to retain their own regional autonomy despite their common ethno-religious heritage. The result was that these separate kingdoms and ethnic groups in Tibetan regions were not politically and militarily allied under the command of the Lhasa government.

In addition to these rather singular domestic political structures, foreign policy was conceived and implemented locally, as attested by local rulers' relationships with China. The relationship between central Tibet and China in the early twentieth century illustrates this point, and a perspective well known to the Labrang Tibetans:

> The Ch'ing and the Tibetans saw the relationship between the emperor and the Dalai Lama from two very different perspectives. From the Ch'ing point of view, the Dalai Lama was a mighty ecclesiastic and a holy being, but nonetheless the emperor's protege. From

the Tibetan point of view, the emperor was merely the Lama's secular patron. This meant that in Tibetan eyes the Dalai Lama's position was superior to that of the Ch'ing emperor.[14]

The ancient Tibetan system of combining religious and political authority in a single person was preserved at Labrang until the Communist period.

The secular authorities at Labrang Monastery maintained a local militia of about three hundred[15] that functioned independently under the leadership of the Alo family, and their forces were supplemented from time to time by alliances with other Tibetans and Chinese troops. Though the Tibetans proved temporarily unable to maintain Labrang's autonomy as a buffer region between the Chinese commanders in Lanzhou and the Ma family's Hui soldiers from 1925 to 1927, they managed to maintain control of the region from 1927 until 1949.

The success of Labrang Monastery was largely due to a combination of factors. Its location, its marketplaces, its being an icon of Tibetan identity for the local people, all contributed to enrich the monastery. Like other monasteries and religious institutions, it soon acquired substantial lands through offerings or by purchase, and collected taxes for use of those lands. Labrang's landholdings and affiliated monasteries were extensive; most of northeastern Tibet felt its influence. Labrang's affiliated monasteries enabled the mother monastery to expand in physical size and regional influence.[16] These monasteries were located in Gansu, Qinghai, and Sichuan, including as far south as Songpan and north in Mongolia, and fell into three loosely defined categories. The first and largest category included townships that were often built up around a monastery or temple, supported by both the sedentary population and the nomads in the area, thus increasing the tax base. The second category comprised monasteries which retained resident religious authorities from Labrang Monastery but whose relationship to Labrang was only religious—there were no political or military representatives in residence at this type of monastery. The last category comprised strictly religiously affiliated monasteries that merely recognized the religious authority of Labrang but were without resident authorities. Though far from ideal or consistent, these categories demonstrate Labrang's at least minimally efficient political bureaucracy.

Labrang Monastery played a role in the history and cultural heritage of Tibet, Mongolia, China, and Muslim parts of China largely because of its location at the borders of those nations. This book provides a glimpse of the fully functioning monastery in its original cultural context and its impact on its neighbors. This is not merely a tale of a sleepy, secluded monastery in a remote place, but an exciting story of adventure and change—an eye-catching account of the events and forces that shaped part of modern Asia. A close and critical look at the historical interactions and conflicts between the different political and ethnic groups in Labrang and the surrounding regions helps to explain the events and circumstances that led to the incorporation of Labrang and the surrounding Tibetan and Muslim Hui regions into the People's Republic of China. This account presents the events at Labrang in the chaotic years of the early twentieth century from the perspective of the Labrang Tibetans; it is certain that other ethnic perspectives will present these events in different ways.

In summary, this book seeks to give readers an accurate portrait of Labrang and its peoples, letting the sources speak for themselves on issues of ethnicity, political sovereignty, and nationalism. Chapter I offers a brief description of Labrang and its historical contexts. Labrang Monastery traces its political and religious roots to central Tibet. Several of its temples and meeting halls followed the models of those found in central Tibet, and Labrang maintained connections with the Lhasa religious hierarchy throughout its history. Chapter II describes the Tibetans, the Chinese, and the Muslim Hui of the region, emphasizing Labrang as a border area, close to a major trade route and, at the same time, a remote repository of esoteric Tibetan Buddhist culture at the edge of the Tibetan Plateau. Tibetans, like others in this cultural matrix of peoples with strong and different ethnic, political, and religious backgrounds, asserted their national character at Labrang.

Chapter III contains the story of the Griebenow family and summarizes their nearly twenty-seven years in northeastern Tibet. Marion and Blanche Griebenow were two young Americans who grew up in the isolation and idealism of pre-World War I United States. They, like many others, were made aware by the war of the worlds beyond North America. Chapter IV presents a brief sketch of the Alo clan, which had a leading role in both the politics and religion at Labrang. Because of the family's leadership roles their story is crucial to the modern history of Labrang, its territories, and all of Amdo.

Chapter V provides a brief account of the region's tumultuous history in the first half of the twentieth century, and it provides a glimpse of similar communities on the Tibetan-Chinese border. Chapter VI describes the attempts to develop the educational systems at Labrang and in its territories and the sentiments toward education among the Labrang Tibetans and their leaders. Chapter VII provides a commentary on the written and photographic materials and includes reflections on the politics and demography of Labrang Monastery and its territories, and in particular, the major cohesive role of religion at Labrang.

*Young Labrang monks
with ceremonial horns.*

I.

LABRANG IN HISTORY:

THE MONASTERY AND THE REGION

L abrang Monastery is located in the Amdo region of Tibet, more specifically in what Tibetans refer to as Khagya Tsodru (*Kha rgya tsho drug*). Amdo occupies the northeast corner of the Tibetan Plateau, north of the steep valleys and high passes of Kham, and east of the high Northern Plains of Tibet. Most of Amdo, including the Labrang region, averages over 10,000 feet above sea level, and has the severe climate and unique vegetation, animal life, and ecosystem peculiar to high-altitude environments. The monastery itself is located at about 8,400 feet (2,820 meters) above sea level. The Labrang region of Amdo borders on China, Muslim territories and Mongolia. It is also near the Hexi Corridor section of the ancient "Silk Road," the main conduit for economic, military, and cultural exchanges between Asia and Europe.

The Griebenows and all foreign visitors marvelled at the variety and numbers of animal and plant species in Amdo and Labrang. It was a wild, rugged land, in this respect analogous to the early North American "Wild West," or Alaska. Untapped and seemingly unlimited resources in remote places with severe climates populated by tough, intensely territorial mountain people with a strange religious culture all gave an exotic image to the Labrang region of Amdo in the eyes of foreign visitors.

Labrang Monastery's natural setting is indeed striking. It is located in a high valley that descends from the 18,000-foot-high glacier-capped peaks that surround the Tibetan plateau. The upper passes are narrow, but they widen into high plateaus with grassy plains suitable for livestock in the summer months. Valleys below the tree line separate into forests that teemed with wildlife in the first half of the twentieth century. Labrang Monastery itself stands in a relatively narrow, winding valley amidst fields of barley and tall grasses once surrounded by evergreen forests. In the early twentieth century neighboring regions were accessible only by narrow trails along steep gorges; there were no roads to Labrang until 1940. The Labrang valley continues to twist down in elevation to the northeast, finally ending in the Yellow River lowlands in nearby China. Nearly all sources describe the descent along this valley as a place where the culture obviously changes from Tibetan to Chinese. This cultural geography confirms the comment that most Tibetans live on the Tibetan Plateau and the Chinese prefer the lower elevations, each choosing the environment more conducive to the maintenance of their cultures and lifestyles.[17]

The Amdo region boasts many rivers, including the Dri Chu (*'Bri chu*)/Yangtze and the Ma Chu/Yellow rivers. The

The Amnye Machen highlands south of Labrang, gateway to the Tibetan Plateau.

Yellow River valley passes through the center of the Labrang region, from the Ragya Monastery down to the confluence of the Yellow and Sangchu/Xiahe rivers, not far from Labrang Monastery and modern-day Lanzhou. This region contained the greatest number of monasteries in Amdo, including Labrang.

The monastery itself, by far the largest and most influential political and religious institution in Amdo in the first half of this century, is located on the Sangchu/Xiahe River, a tributary of the Yellow River, on the Xiahe or Kalawat Plateau, just south of the Hui market town of Linxia. It is about 103 kilometers from Linxia, and about 285 kilometers west-southwest from Lanzhou, the capital city of Gansu Province. There were trails to the other border towns, Chone (Choni) and Songpan to the south, to the Tibetan highlands to the west and southwest, to Kumbum, other monasteries and Xining city to the northwest, to local towns east of Labrang, and to Lanzhou.

Few accurate population statistics exist for Labrang in the early twentieth century, much less for earlier times. Apa Alo, the local leader during the Griebenow mission, describing Amdo in the early twentieth century, gives some at least approximate data:

> Amdo consists of about two million square kilometers of territory, is surrounded by mountains, notably the Amnye Machen mountains. According to estimates made in the 1930s there were about 600 ethnic groups in Amdo. The political structure can be roughly described as a regionally variable mixture of large estates or small kingdoms with inherited titles and powers, towns built up around major monasteries, and open, unsettled territories claimed by groups of nomads. There were altogether about one and a half million people in Amdo. Buddhism was the primary religion.[18]

Labrang Monastery was an important Tibetan cultural center and an important trading center located at a strategic intersection of major ethnic groups.

Labrang's Cultural Heritage

The Tibetan Buddhists describe the Sangchu valley in poetic terms. The valley is visualized as more than just a valley; the eight Buddhist auspicious signs[19] and the seven attributes of royalty[20] are implicit in the mountain peaks, and in the twisting, forested valleys, rivers, and high plains. Certainly this sense of inspiration from the environment is not misplaced, nor is the image of a jewel of Buddhist dharma in a remote high-altitude mountain valley, since Labrang Monastery was a major center of Tibetan religious culture, with a rich and distinctive heritage. The enchanting image is reinforced by the predictions which the Tibetans find in classical Indian Buddhist literature about Buddhism coming to Labrang.[21] These visions and predictions have been living for centuries in Amdo's religious history and cultural imagination.

A Tibetan woman relaxes on the wooden bridge that crossed the Sangchu River near the Gungthang stūpa.

Long before Labrang Monastery was founded, Amdo's culture was diverse: Chinese Buddhism from the Tang Dynasty courts had considerable influence in the region, the pre-Buddhist Tibetan Bon religion was established throughout Amdo, and in the ninth and tenth centuries new influences from central Tibet took root in Amdo. As Amdo developed political and trade links with the Chinese and the Mongols, and when Labrang was founded in the early eighteenth

The offering of a "torma" (gtor rgyag). A uniquely Tibetan Buddhist ritual which was very common at Labrang. This is a remarkably elaborate version of the ritual, with the musical accompaniment of long horns played by opulently dressed trumpeters, drummers and cymbalists. The master of ceremonies ('cham dpon) sits in front of the triangular structure in the center in preparation for lighting a ritual fire. His attendant is at his right and other young attendants carry smaller tormas and incense burners in front of the main shrine. There is a lay audience in the foreground. The main "torma" precedes this group.

century, it became a major conduit for Tibetan Buddhist culture to Mongolia. All of these diverse influences contributed to make Labrang Monastery evolve into a dynamic cultural, religious, economic, and political environment.[22]

The historical beginnings of Labrang are interesting because they evolve out of one of the most important periods of Tibetan civilization. The Fifth Dalai Lama, Nawang Losang Gyatso (1617-1682), is linked to Labrang through his 1653 meeting with the First Jamyang Shaypa (1648-1721), then a precocious five-year-old who was to become the founder of Labrang Monastery. This meeting took place while the Dalai Lama was in Amdo en route to a diplomatic meeting with the Chinese.[23] Years later, the Fifth Dalai Lama was to confer full ordination on Jamyang Shaypa in Lhasa, when the novice was twenty-seven years old.[24]

After receiving full ordination Jamyang Shaypa devoted some twenty-five years to the rigorous study of Buddhist scriptures, including the full range of Buddhist philosophies, psychologies, and mystical subjects. He mastered the ritual arts, ritual dance, and *maṇḍala* science. He studied unflaggingly under the tutelage of numerous scholars and adepts in the major monastic establishments in central Tibet, concentrating on the Kadampa and Gelukpa teachings. It is said that he became very austere, thin and frail.[25]

Meanwhile, the capable Fifth Dalai Lama kept the Tibetan political world in a rather delicate balance. An astute political negotiator, the Fifth Dalai Lama visited China in 1651-53, keeping Tibet's imperial eastern neighbor at bay through prudent diplomacy, and at the same time making use of Mongolian assistance to consolidate the central Tibetan realm and absorb western Tibet and Ladakh. The Fifth Dalai Lama's death in 1682 upset the balance in central Tibet. His ministers decided to try to maintain equilibrium in the kingdom by concealing their leader's passing. This deception

New Year's celebration, Assembly Hall (founded 1710, enlarged 1772). The dancers personify the deities invoked in dramatic representations of the defeat of evil, often including episodes from Tibetan history. These photographs show that Tibetan "cham" ('cham) dancing was accessible to the public. The ritual dance involves elaborate preparations, prayers, and offerings, real and imagined. Marion Griebenow wrote an extensive description of the 1934 New Year's celebration: "As soon as the New Year celebrations are over, guests begin to gather for the first great festival of the year, the Monlam, or Great Prayer, held from the thirteenth to the sixteenth day of the first moon. On the first day a great silk idol is placed out on the hillside. Offerings are presented after which the silk image is folded up and returned to the monastery. Dancers come out into a ring of spectators on the second day of the festival, and dance to the music of a band of drums, cymbals, and horns, which keep up a constant noise. This dance, which is the main feature of the festival, is in four divisions and lasts all day. On the third day there is nothing but a crowded bazaar until after dark when the full moon rises. Then the great butter images are put on display all about the main chanting hall. These are illuminated by torches carried in the hands of men, and are very pretty in their various colors and much glitter. Since many of the images are ten feet high or more, it takes hundreds of pounds of butter to fashion one of them." M.G. Griebenow, "Tibetan Religious Festivals," The Alliance Weekly (22 September 1934): 600ff.

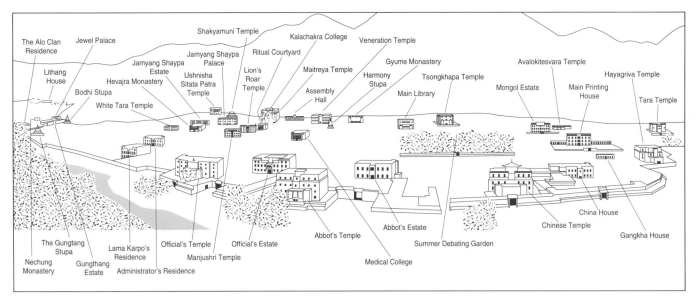

The Alo Clan Residence
Jewel Palace
Shakyamuni Temple
Kalachakra College
Veneration Temple
Jamyang Shaypa Palace
Ritual Courtyard
Jamyang Shaypa Estate
Lithang House
Gyume Monastery
Maitreya Temple
Harmony Stupa
Avalokitesvara Temple
Hevajra Monastery
Lion's Roar Temple
Tsongkhapa Temple
Hayagriva Temple
Ushnisha Sitata Patra Temple
Assembly Hall
Main Library
Mongol Estate
Main Printing House
Bodhi Stupa
White Tara Temple
Tara Temple
China House
The Gungtang Stupa
Chinese Temple
Gangkha House
Lama Karpo's Residence
Official's Temple
Official's Estate
Abbot's Estate
Nechung Monastery
Gungthang Estate
Manjushri Temple
Abbot's Temple
Summer Debating Garden
Administrator's Residence
Medical College

Labrang Monastery, ca. 1932

lasted until 1697, during which time Jamyang Shaypa played a part in the central Tibetan government's attempts to maintain stability. Jamyang Shaypa participated in the ordination ceremony of the Sixth Dalai Lama at Tashilhunpo Monastery in Shigatse in 1697, but with young Tsangyang Gyatso's rejection of his monastic vows and his position as Sixth Dalai Lama, the subsequent occupation of Lhasa by the Dzungar Mongols in 1705, and the Sixth Dalai Lama's flight in 1706, central Tibet was in turmoil. Jamyang Shaypa left an unstable political environment in Lhasa when he accepted the Mongolian invitation to found a monastery in remote Amdo.[26]

His 1695 meeting with the local Khoshud Mongol Prince Erdeni Jinong, known in Chinese as the "Henan Qinwang" (Prince of the Henan district)[27] and in Tibetan as the "Sogpo Gyalpo," and several local Tibetan families marks the original conception of Labrang. Though he had initially declined the request, in 1709 Jamyang Shaypa finally went to Amdo to establish a monastery.[28] Thus it came to pass that the Amdo-born Khenpo Losang Gyaltsen, or the First Jamyang Shaypa, went back to his original home in Amdo from Drepung Monastery's Gomang College,[29] and brought Labrang Monastery from its humble beginnings in a tent to its development as a major community institution.

Part of the complex twentieth-century governance of Labrang originated and evolved from the thirteenth-century Mongols Genghis and Khubilai Khan, who initiated the connection of Mongol khans to Tibetan lamas. This connection was continued by the seventeenth-century Mongol ruler Gushri Khan, who invaded Tibet to assist the Fifth Dalai Lama. Gushri Khan's grandson was the locally influential Prince Erdeni Jinong, the "Henan Qinwang," the highest-ranking nobleman of the Khoshud Mongols in Amdo.

The Mongol Henan Qinwang was the preeminent ruler in Amdo south of the Ma Chu/Yellow River.[30] (In Chinese *he* means "river" and *nan* means "south.") His descendant in power in the 1920s and 1930s was the "Mongolian Prince," Kunga Paljor, one of the twenty-nine Mongol princes in Amdo.[31] As the highest ranking Mongolian prince, his influence extended even over parts of Gansu, Qinghai and Sichuan, including the region around Lake Kokonor (*Kokenuur*). Kunga Paljor died in 1940 and his wife Lukho and daughter Tashi Tsering ruled[32] until Tashi Tsering married Amgon, or Kalsang Dondrup, Apa Alo's son and the nephew of Jamyang Shaypa.

By the early eighteenth century, the Mongol tribes had largely adopted Tibetan language, lifestyles, and religion. Of all the peoples present in the region the Mongols enjoyed the strongest sense of solidarity and peaceful coexistence with the Tibetans. This was doubtless the result of the Mongol sponsorship of the monastery and the Mongols' faith in Tibetan Buddhism. The local Mongols, with a royal palace located at Labrang, were responsible for financing much of the original construction of Labrang Monastery in the early eighteenth century and maintained significant but gradually declining political influence through the period of the Griebenow Mission. The approximately 15,000 Mongol subjects[33] in the modern period lived primarily in the Labrang territories and recognized the religious and secular authority of Labrang Monastery as endorsed by the Mongol Prince.

The monastery's formal name is Gandan Shaydrup Dargyay Tashi Gyaysu Khyilway Ling (*dGe ldan bshad sgrub dar rgyas bkra shis gyas su 'khyil ba'i gling*), but it is most commonly known as Labrang Tashi Khyil or simply Labrang. A "labrang" is actually a Tibetan teacher's personal property. It may include religious books and materials as well as buildings, land, wealth, and even tax revenues. Labrang was the "labrang" of the lineage of the Jamyang Shaypas.[34] After the death of the First Jamyang Shaypa, the

Second through Fourth Jamyang Shaypas inherited, or more accurately, continued the lineage of Jamyang Shaypas in their office (i.e., their "labrang") at Labrang. The Tibetans believed that these boys were enlightened or powerful beings, the living emanations of the First Jamyang Shaypa.

The actual date of the founding of Labrang Monastery was planned to coincide with the 300th anniversary of Tsong-khapa's founding of Ganden Monastery in central Tibet.[35] Its beginnings were modest—a large tent located on the site where the main assembly hall would be built, with a congregation of five monks. The hall was built in 1711 using that of Drepung Monastery in central Tibet as a model.[36] The monastery grew over the years to include well over one hundred buildings, accommodating its population of between 3,000 and 5,000 monks, depending on the time of year. By the twentieth century there were

> six *Sūtra* Halls, forty-eight Buddha temples, thirty-one palaces for the Jamyang Shaypas and the senior Lamas, thirty mansions for the incarnate Lamas, eight government buildings, six big kitchens, one printing house, two main meeting halls, over five hundred prayer-wheel rooms, and more than five hundred common monks' cells.[37]

Over the years the monastery grew slowly not only in its physical size, but also in terms of its political mechanisms and its role in Amdo. The Second Jamyang Shaypa (1728-1791) was installed as leader of Labrang only after overcoming disputes over his legitimate claim to the title. He prevailed, was ordained by the famous scholar Jangkya Rolpay Dorje, and made significant contributions to the monastery. The Second Jamyang Shaypa enlarged Labrang's existing structures and sponsored the construction of new buildings, among them the Kalachakra Temple (1763) and the Medical College (1784). He was also the first Jamyang Shaypa to hold the position of abbot of nearby Kumbum Monastery for one term, a practice that was followed by the later Jamyang Shaypas.

Like his predecessors, the Third Jamyang Shaypa (1792-1856) was a native of the region. His identity was established early in his life, after which he began his monastic studies and training. He was ordained in Lhasa by the Panchen Lama in 1812. The Third Jamyang Shaypa was known for his ascetic practices. He followed the *Vinaya* rules strictly and exemplified the Buddhist teachings on humility and moral conduct. He always found time to help even novice monks in their studies and would assist them in the most menial tasks. He became famous for his ability to maintain a stable state of meditation, even while travelling on horseback. Though he did not undertake much new construction to the monastic complex at Labrang, he oversaw the completion of the Medical College begun by his predecessor.

The Fourth Jamyang Shaypa (1856-1916), a native of Kham, was different from the other Jamyang Shaypas in that he travelled extensively to solicit funds for new structures at Labrang. He was educated at Labrang and in Lhasa. In 1881 he built a major religious structure at Labrang, the Hevajra Temple, and in 1898 made a historically important diplomatic visit to the Buddhist community at Wutai Shan in China.

The Fifth Jamyang Shaypa, second son of Gonpo Dondrup of the locally significant Alo family, was born in 1916 and died on April 14, 1947. His full name was Losang Jamyang Yeshe Tenpay Gyaltsan Palzang Po (also known as Palshul Nawang Tsondru; in Chinese, Huang Zhengguang).[38] He was unique as a child and was identified as the reincarnation of the Fourth Jamyang Shaypa in 1919 by the interregnal Regent of Labrang, the Ninth Panchen Lama.[39] His family arrived at Labrang on August 6, 1919, and he was enthroned at age five.[40]

The Alo family: Apa Alo; his father, Gonpo Dondrup; Balmang Tsang; the Fifth Jamyang Shaypa; Guru lHatso; Khyenrab Dondrup; Amgon.

Labrang Monastery, elevation 8,400 feet (2,720 meters), located in the high Sangchu River (Xiahe) valley on the Muslim and Chinese borders. It supported over three thousand monks and was an important crossroads for trade between China, Xinjiang, Tibet, and Mongolia. Tibetan records describe the valley's geological formations in the shape of the eight auspicious symbols—conch, umbrella, victory banner, fish, vase, wheel, knot of infinity, and lotus.

The Fifth Jamyang Shaypa's older brother, Apa Alo, was the most important military figure in the area. He led the Tibetan militia and forged an independent claim to authority with the aid of Chinese military and political figures. His authority derived from his gradual rise to political power and was legitimated by his younger brother's status as incarnate lama of Labrang Monastery, who, at least according to the Tibetan tradition, was the final authority in religious and secular matters at Labrang Monastery and in all of its territories.

The Fifth Jamyang Shaypa's 1919 entry into Labrang was a grand affair; the Rinpoche (the "Reverend") and his entourage stopped en route at many regional monasteries and encampments, and were greeted in Labrang by about one thousand troops of the predominantly Hui Ninghai Army bearing gifts from the Qinghai authorities (Ninghai was the name given to the local Chinese Republican forces in the Ningxia-Qinghai area). Nawang Tendhar, the Fifth Jamyang Shaypa's uncle, accepted financial authority for Labrang from the Manager Li Zongzhe (Tibetan: Tsondru Gyatso, *brTson 'grus rgya mtsho*), and Jamyang Shaypa's father, Gonpo Dondrup, assumed political responsibility. The party was met with drums, bells, conches, shawms and long horns. The streets were full of people, all of the monastic officials were present, and "there were tears in the eyes of many."[41] The Alo family—Gonpo Dondrup, his spouse, Apa Alo, and the rest of his children—were very well received by the Mongol Prince.[42] Further, Pei Zhenjun, the army general of Lanzhou, and Zhu Geliang,[43] representing the Chinese Republican authorities in Lanzhou, came to honor the arrival of Jamyang Shaypa. Local rulers sent representatives as well.

It is not surprising, therefore, that the Alo family was given special status as the protector and vessel of the incarnate precious one, the Rinpoche, or in the local dialect, "Alak." When the family arrived at Labrang, its already dynamic history took yet another major turn with the gaining of religious and political prestige in Labrang. It was this family of authorities that allowed permanent residence to a foreign Christian mission and family, the Griebenows. Marion Griebenow was about twenty-two and Blanche about twenty-three when they started their mission at Labrang. Jamyang Shaypa entered the monastic system as successor to his inherited throne in 1919, and was about six years old when the Griebenows arrived.

The current Sixth Jamyang Shaypa is Jetsun Losang Jigme Tubten Chogyi Nyima Palzang Po (*rJe btsun blo bzang 'jigs med thub bstan chos kyi nyi ma dpal bzang po*), identified after the Chinese took control of Amdo in 1950. The monastery and community were largely destroyed by officially sponsored vandalism in the 1950s and mid-1960s, and further damaged by fire in the 1980s. But these are later chapters in Labrang's history.

Labrang's governance has at various times been under the military and political control of the Mongol Princes, the Hui militarists and regional Tibetan leaders. Until the Chinese Communist era, however, daily administration at Labrang was primarily in the hands of the Labrang Tibetans, regardless of the battles with the Qinghai troops and the claims of the Chinese. Its location and turbulent political history have created Mongol, Muslim Hui and Chinese enclaves in the area, creating a mosaic of cultures on their shared borders. This account, a necessarily brief unravelling of the tightly wound patterns of cultures, religions, and politics in Labrang and Amdo, aims to provide an overview of the complex cultural identifications, changes, peaceful cooperation, and bloody conflicts that took place at Labrang between 1700 and 1950.[44]

Tibetans in typical dress at Labrang.

II.

THE ETHNIC MATRIX:
TIBETANS, CHINESE, AND MUSLIMS

Any accurate description of Labrang Monastery is necessarily as much about the Tibetan people as it is about the monastery; indeed, being Tibetan is to be part of its unique religious and cultural heritage. Labrang was a focal point of Tibetan cultural heritage. This was very apparent to the Griebenows, and is noted on numerous occasions in their memoirs. The American missionaries remarked on several occasions that the boundaries of Tibetan culture and Tibetan territory were distinctive, and hardly subjects for dispute. The Labrang Tibetans differed from their neighbors in language, lifestyles, religion, and ethical sensibility. Who were these Tibetans? And who were their neighbors? The following description summarizes the cultural heritage and social classes in the Labrang region. This survey seeks to present a unique culture, not built on a blueprint of neighboring culture, but Labrang's own—a Tibetan border culture.

Tibetan literary sources identify the Labrang Tibetans as descendants of one of four major clans of Tibetan peoples,[45] and explain their presence in Amdo as military protectors of the Tibetan-Chinese border, sent from central Tibet in the ninth century during the period of the Tibetan Empire.[46] Later Tibetans also came to Labrang to trade and to be in the presence of the Jamyang Shaypas. The early history

given here is plausible in light of the well-known fact that the ancient Tibetan empire extended far beyond what is now called Labrang and Amdo. For example, two of the several important Tibetan kingdoms in the region in the preceding centuries were Tsongkha, well-established until 904, and the better-known Xixia empire (also known as Tangut, or Minyak) (ca. 990-1227). Founded by a Tibeto-Burman border people, the Xixia empire was heavily influenced by Buddhism.[47] In Labrang and Amdo the currents of Tibetan history run deep.

Labrang has been at times simultaneously described as part of Mongolia, Tibet, Qinghai, and Gansu. The irony here is that while Labrang and its territories never moved in the minds of the people of Labrang, claims of ownership by larger military and political groups have changed significantly.[48] The region has been Tibetan since the seventh century, and according to the Tibetans, throughout recorded history.[49] The Chinese presence in Amdo in general was always ineffective, nominal, and transient. Tibetans were proud of their identity as Tibetans, and valued their sense of national history with its mythical heroes and villains.

One of the problems in the Labrang territory is that even though the region has such a distinctive heritage, the historical, folkloric, and literary Tibetan names of the boundaries in and around Labrang unfortunately have done little to clearly define the area. Given the national pride of Tibetans in general and the independence of diverse groups of nomads in particular, in addition to their literary history and cultural imagination, it is not surprising that Tibetan scholars cite conflicting territorial divisions and boundaries.[50] Territories have been renamed when inherited, when taken over by a dominant nomadic group, or when different groups united. Besides Tibetan tribal names, there are also different political and geographical names for these same regions. The local Tibetans and their written records cite different names, but one thing is consistent—all agree that "Amdo" designates all of northeastern ethnic Tibet, and that Labrang is its major cultural center.[51]

The problem of different place-names demonstrates another distinctive characteristic of the Tibetans in general and the Labrang Tibetans in particular—their language. Though in some of the neighboring regions language is secondary to other elements of culture,[52] at Labrang it was an important factor. The Tibetan language of the local Labrang and

Amdo Tibetans is nearly unintelligible to the average Tibetan speaker of central Tibet. Still, the language of Labrang is beyond any doubt a distinctively Tibetan language, closely related to central Tibetan, of the Tibeto-Burman language group. Like many cultures with literary histories and philosophies of language, the Tibetans regard their language as special, particularly since it became a repository of Indian Buddhism.[53]

The cultural heritage of the Labrang Tibetans is as distinctive as their history. Tibetan Buddhist rituals, celebrations, festivals, and holidays were the center of life at Labrang. Tibetan merchants lived in and around the Labrang township, trading wool and agricultural goods for Chinese manufactured goods. In contrast, Tibetan nomads provided the backbone of the Tibetan regional economy. Their seasonal migrations to graze and market their herds of yaks and sheep often brought them to Labrang's markets and monastery, where they did business and at the same time renewed their spiritual ties. The monastery grew over the years and trade flourished well into the twentieth century.

The Tibetan people were themselves categorized based on their social and political status, which varied considerably.[54] In addition to conforming to dominant religious and political institutions, the Tibetans in Labrang and Amdo had very different class or social status—some were free and sometimes property owners, some were tenant farmers, and others were workers and families who spent their entire lives on large estates owned by the monastery or by other independent kingdoms. All of these peoples were divided into local populations or tribes that could be small in number, similar in ways to their neighbors but linguistically and often somewhat culturally distinct, with extended family structures, extensive land claims and property holdings, and hereditary leadership within specific families.

A local Tibetan family who befriended the Griebenows.

Mongolian-style yurts beyond the southeast wall of Labrang. The yurts frame Labrang's Gungthang stūpa.

There were some six hundred (a rough estimate) tribes in the region, but the Tibetan and Chinese sources describe four groups of people at Labrang[55] based on their level of affiliation with Labrang. At first glance, the four seem to be well-defined categories, but on closer inspection, the criteria for inclusion in each category are not so obvious. Western readers must interpret these popular social structures carefully. Still, because the Tibetans use these four categories to describe themselves, I include them here. The first category were the "blessed people" (Tibetan, *lha sde*; Chinese, *shen min*).[56] This group included approximately eleven Mongolian tribes (called "arrows"), thirteen Tibetan villages,[57] and local aristocrats.[58] The former groups were subjects of Labrang Monastery by historical transfer from wealthy aristocrats to the monastery. The people's lands were owned by and their livelihoods contracted to the monastery. Taxes were mandatory, and if a family was unable to pay taxes, service to the monastery could be substituted. The latter peoples included in the category of "blessed people" were Tibetan and Mongolian aristocrats, wealthy people who donated livestock and substantial offerings of goods. It is therefore important to note that the "blessed people" included rich and poor persons, both indentured farmers and herders whose livelihoods were contracted to the monastery and wealthy patrons who retained ownership of their estates. Thus the criteria for inclusion in this classification

Tibetan woman selling cups on market day.

was not wealth, social status, individual autonomy, or education. Briefly, it is rather based on a level of tax commitment and participation in the affairs of the monastery.

The second traditional category of Tibetan tribes affiliated with Labrang Monastery were extended clans of nomads often in isolated regions who asserted their autonomy and independence. Though the nomads migrated with the seasons, their lifestyles and pasturelands were organized in seasonal patterns; they did not wander about entirely at random. The monastery-appointed officials of these territorially circumscribed nomads had local legislative authority, and had at least a nominal commitment to Labrang Monastery.[59] Though based on a particular territory, this group could not claim hereditary ownership of their pasturelands. The third traditional group, by contrast, were landed Tibetan aristocrats whose estates and grazing territories were inherited. These aristocrats governed their own estates, but acknowledged the religious authority of Labrang and provided the monastery regular donations. Unlike the taxes on the first group, the donations of these two groups were not strictly mandatory. Nevertheless, the records show that donations were substantial and regular.

The fourth traditional category of Tibetans affiliated with Labrang Monastery dwelt in and around the predominantly Salar Muslim[60] town of Xunhua, mixed with the Salars and others. This interpenetration of Labrang Tibetans and Salar Muslim peoples is only one example of the widespread mutual interaction of differing ethnic groups, political statuses, linguistic accents and religious allegiances on the Tibetan-Hui-Chinese ethnic borderlands. The relationships between the monastery and its constituents includes a wide variety of tax commitments, marriage ties, and religious bonds. The traditional categories are approximations used for ease of description; the actual makeup of Labrang's social structures was a complex web of economics, politics and religion, description of which goes beyond the limits of this brief introduction.

Ethnic diversity was typical in this border region; the four main Tibetan groups mentioned above included Buddhist, Muslim, and Bonpo religions.[61] There was similar diversity to the northeast in the important Hui center at Linxia-Hezhou, in the territories of the Dongxiang (Mongol-speaking Muslims), and in the Chinese areas. Still, Labrang was itself distinctively Tibetan, a gateway to the high Tibetan plateau. Though Labrang was once claimed by the Mongols, by the Chinese at various times, and by the Xining Hui in the early Republic, the Griebenows and other contemporary sources place Labrang entirely in Tibet, within the ethnic boundary of the Tibetan people, or within the boundaries of places that were part of the eighth-century Tibetan Empire.[62]

One approximation of the population of Labrang (made by uncertain methods) is provided by a Chinese scholar working in the region during the 1930s. He estimated the population in the Labrang district of Amdo to be less than 50,000 persons, consisting of "13,249 villagers, 26,427 tent-dwellers, and 7,640 monks: 47,316 altogether. Of the tent-dwellers, or nomadic pastoralists, 23,227 are Tibetans and 3,200 Tibetanized Mongols."[63] Though these figures have been met with some skepticism, the number of villagers near Labrang seems plausible; the numbers of tent-dwellers or the nomadic population fluctuated with the seasons, since they would be drawn by market-days or religious celebrations at Labrang at certain times of the year, but would otherwise be far away. The number of monks cited here is high, but there may well have been times when these figures were accurate, during Lunar New Year, or because of teachings to be given by visiting lamas attracting large audiences.[64]

The cantor (oṁ mdzad) of the main monastery, with a stern expression.

These statistics, while unverifiable, nevertheless show that the Buddhist monastic presence was very strong and that sedentary lay Tibetans were mostly farmers and merchants. The nomads were quite different and easily recognized from

"With friends after a Chinese feast given by a White Russian friend, Mr. Gorohoff." M.G. Griebenow, the first month of Spring, 1932. Third from left, Adjutant Li; Mr. Gorohoff; in the rear, M.G. Griebenow; center front, County Magistrate Xi; to the right, Apa Alo; Postmaster Jin; an unidentified merchant; far right, militia Section Chief Yu.

their encampments, their dress, and their mobile lifestyle. Additionally, the Mongols, most of whom were nomads, were a distinguishable presence at Labrang, though very much in the minority.

Moreover, the proximity of Labrang to the Chinese border made political and military relations between the Tibetans and the local Chinese authorities necessary and frequent.

Gonpo Dondrup, the patriarch of the ruling Tibetan Alo family at Labrang, was employed by Zhao Erfeng in the first decade of the twentieth century while the family lived in Litang, which provided the patriarch with important experience and connections with the Chinese. The relations between the Chinese and Tibetans were favorable for the Alos in later years, and given the persistent trouble with the Salars and Hui Muslims, being able to invoke defense agreements with the Chinese was a distinct advantage for the Tibetans until the late 1940s.

The Griebenows and other missionaries and travellers often referred to the Labrang communities as "Tibet," and their maps include Labrang within the boundaries of Tibet. The missionaries based their judgment on their perceptions of the land, its peoples and cultures. They did not have detailed knowledge of the regional history; they likely thought it irrelevant. To them Labrang was a remote, high-altitude environment inhabited by Tibetans who had a distinctive and complex culture unlike anything in the vicinity. It had been described to them as "Tibet" prior to their arrival and was regarded as such by the local people they encountered. However, the Griebenows' simple definition has become the subject of controversy. The modern debate over Tibetan boundaries challenges the validity of the Griebenows' assumptions based on criteria for state and nationhood, ethnicity, historical treaties and international law. A comprehensive study of the legal boundaries of Tibet is an enormous project that goes far beyond the limits of this book. Suffice it to say that this book presents important data for the history of the Tibetan nation.

The Chinese

The Chinese presence in Labrang was evident on several levels. Labrang monastic officials and leaders of the Tibetan militia had contact with Chinese officials from nearby Lanzhou. In addition to the periodic visits by Chinese politicians and military, Chinese entrepreneurs provided the community with manufactured goods, craftsmen, building contractors, and contacts with the outside world—postal service, and the routes out of Tibet and China.

The Ming, Qing, and Communist Chinese empires all played important roles in the history of Labrang and Amdo. The Ming emperors stationed troops in nearby towns like Lanzhou and Xining, and appointed local Tibetans as regional leaders. When the Ming Dynasty fell to the Manchu Qing emperor in 1644, the Manchus introduced a new administrative system and a new vision of China's relationship to Tibet and Mongolia. The new administration involved a range of Manchu institutions establishing varying degrees of control throughout China. In those areas they inherited from the Ming, traditional Chinese institutions were preserved. The new vision reformulated the classical Chinese theory of the centrality of China, the authority of the Manchu emperors, and the relationships between China and the nations on its borders. Labrang Monastery was considered to lie inside the Chinese empire, though Chinese authority throughout the territories it claimed was intermittent and often negligible.

The fall of the Qing Dynasty in 1911 and subsequent rise of regional "warlords" only exacerbated conditions in Gansu and, for that matter, all of China. From 1911 to 1928 in eastern China, and until much later elsewhere, independent leaders with personal armies strove for control, most often solely motivated by wishes to increase their own power, wealth, and territorial control.

While the Chinese central government was in turmoil, the boundary lines between social classes, lifestyles, and tribal groups in the Labrang region were evolving and becoming more sharply defined. For example:

> At the Gansu frontier, local variation within Chinese culture is muted, if not overwhelmed, by the fundamental contrast between sedentary agriculture and pastoral nomadism, between the cultures of Us and Them.[65]

Muslim merchants in Labrang's marketplace, offering items for sale to the general Tibetan population.

The animosity between the Muslims and Chinese was also preserved from years past:

> History reveals that Han hatred of the Muslims, the shortsightedness of the Ch'ing rulers, and the narrow-mindedness of the Ch'ing Muslims in building their own kingdoms within China were responsible for the deaths of 12,000,000 Muslims and an equal or larger number of Han Chinese.[66]

Perhaps the warfare and chaos made a settlement of the conflict between the Hui and the Tibetans impossible for the Chinese. The Chinese authorities in Gansu did little to deter Qinghai's Hui government from posting a garrison at Labrang from 1924 to 1927. In Chinese politics, which were to affect Labrang, 1927 and the following several years were tumultuous. Chiang Kai-shek (Jiang Jieshi) set up his Nationalist power base in Nanjing, but after a long and bloody struggle temporarily defeated the Communists. The warlord General Feng Yuxiang, the famous "Christian General" known for the strict discipline and high standards of conduct of his troops, made the fateful decision to follow the Nationalists.[67] Meanwhile, other military groups fought among themselves throughout China.

The Chinese have always been among the Labrang Tibetans' closest neighbors and strongest trade partners, and have been by turns both military allies and enemies. Their influence at Labrang throughout the centuries has nonetheless been muted by mutual agreement and deep-rooted ethnic differences. Though the Chinese clearly included Labrang in their vision of their empire, and at times members of the Alo clan acted as functionaries of different Chinese governments, the sources for the present book assert that the relationship between the Chinese and Tibetan leadership in the early twentieth century was one of mutual recognition and respect. The Chinese governments made claims to ultimate sovereignty over Labrang, and over the rest of Tibet, but did not dare to enforce these claims.

The Muslims—Hui, Salars, Merchants, Soldiers, and Nomads

In addition to the influence of Tibetan Buddhist political and religious establishments and Chinese economic and military strength, Muslim peoples—Salar, Dongxiang, and Hui, for example—have had a strong and stormy history at Labrang. These groups established an important religious and trading center about 103 kilometers northeast of Labrang

in modern-day Linxia-Hezhou. Linxia originally was the major market town, but Linxia and Hezhou had merged into one place by the modern period and maintain an important presence in Labrang's marketplaces to the present day. Hui farmers, sedentary traders, and even nomads from regions near Linxia, Xunhua, and Xining tended their crops and herds in the plains alongside their Tibetan neighbors and traded their goods in Labrang's markets. They were the primary brokers of goods between the Tibetan and Mongolian nomads and the Chinese.

Muslim merchants established themselves east of the Pamir range as early as the eighth century, but trading centers were not well-established in the Amdo region until the nineteenth century. In addition to trade and agriculture, some of these peoples had lifestyles very similar to those of the Tibetan nomads. All shared a strong sense of connection to their homelands and clan loyalty to regional warlords or generals. In the early twentieth century, the most stable and enduring Hui warlord clan was the Ma family, who claimed a lineage of fourteen patriarchs. Ma Qi was beginning his rise as commander of the local Hui-dominated military force. His brother Ma Lin and Ma Bufang, designated "governors" of Qinghai, continued to harass Labrang after 1927, albeit ineffectively, until the 1940s.[68] Yet the Ma clan was unfortunately not unified with the other important local Hui leaders outside of the Qinghai region. This became a contributing cause to the eventual military defeat of both the Qinghai and Gansu Muslims in the early and middle twentieth century. The Muslim power base closest to Labrang was at Linxia, with connections to Salars and Hui in Xunhua and Xining. The Xining Hui under the Ma family were perhaps the most frequent antagonists of the Tibetans but for various reasons—Labrang's important markets and its connections to wide-ranging Chinese interests chief among them, and the opposition of the Chinese forces

Tibetans on the move. Skillful riders, these Tibetans carry poles for ritual flags, possibly en route to a ceremony to control earth spirits.

in Gansu—Labrang did not suffer the worst treatment at the hands of Hui Muslim and Chinese regional warlords. Some semblance of stability prevailed at Labrang, although not without periodic crises, including the Ma family's military occupation of Labrang from 1924 to 1927.

Islam has been a powerful component of Hui cultural identity certainly on the level of a "public theology," much as Buddhism is for the Tibetan Buddhists. This factor kept the Muslim Hui, for the most part, separate from the Buddhist Tibetans and their Buddhist-Confucian-Daoist Chinese neighbors. Though this is the case, it should also be kept in mind that there were and are both Tibetan Muslims and Han Chinese converts to Islam.

> Negative Han [Chinese] assumptions, often codified in law and almost always enforced in custom, had altered but not eliminated Muslim resistance to assimilation. Many Sino-Muslims, or Hui, maintained their identity with energy, asserting their own points of superiority over the Han. They did this despite a high level of material and linguistic acculturation, despite a tradition of male-Hui/female-Han intermarriage that eroded their Central Asian physical characteristics, even despite a consciousness of *belonging*.[69]

Another group, the Salar Muslims, were centered just northwest of Labrang, along the Yellow River, from Xining south of the river in the Huangzhong region up to Labrang territory. These tribal groups were farmers, and maintained a town at Xunhua. There were about 50,000 Salars with sixty-two mosques in the region during the Griebenow mission.[70] Many descriptions of the interrelations between cultural identity and political authority apply to the different groups of Salars and other Muslims as well as to the Labrang Tibetans, with the addition of consistent and fierce hostilities between Muslim groups and with the Qing, Nationalist, and Communist governments.[71] These hostilities were taking place in the same regions and times as the development of Labrang and its territories in the early twentieth century, and at the same time as the Griebenow mission.

In the years after 1928, the relations of the Qinghai Hui under Ma Bufang with the Labrang Tibetans were volatile and sometimes explosive. Apa Alo made consistent efforts to resist them on several fronts. He appealed to Chinese authorities through the decades for support against the Hui, and he enlisted the support of the neighboring tribes also hostile to Ma family rule, for example the Golok nomads to the south. Alo established and maintained a garrison of about three hundred Tibetan militiamen, albeit primitively armed, and finally made consistent efforts to negotiate with the Hui. Nevertheless, disputes with the Hui continued through the 1930s and, though somewhat less frequently, through the 1940s.

A frequent visitor to the Griebenow household.

III.

STRANGERS FROM ABROAD:

THE GRIEBENOWS AND
THEIR CHRISTIAN MISSION AT LABRANG

The sponsor of the Griebenow mission, the Christian and Missionary Alliance (CMA), was active in the Amdo region from about 1896 to 1949. There were several missionaries who dared to visit Labrang for brief periods before the Griebenows, but they were always in danger, for they were considered to be heretics and trouble-makers by the Tibetans and by the neighboring Muslims. Though it was established elsewhere along the Chinese border, the CMA was not permanently established at Labrang until the Griebenow mission, which lasted from 1922 to 1949.

One of the first CMA missionaries to visit Labrang was William Christie,[72] who was also one of the people who captivated M.G.'s (Marion Grant Griebenow preferred to be called by his initials) imagination and inspired him to join the CMA. Though he was treated extremely harshly, Christie's experiences and trials generated interest in Tibet. His story is typical of those of many missionaries of this era. In 1892 he heard Rev. A.B. Simpson, the founder of the Christian and Missionary Alliance, speak about his own determination to evangelize Tibet.[73] Christie was fascinated, and at age twenty-two resolved to carry the Christian message to that remote country. Though his years in China's

Christian "evangelical fields" were particularly stormy, and though he frequently had to flee from communities hostile to his work, he was the first CMA missionary to establish a presence in the China mission field. He began his attempts to spread the Gospels in 1896 in Minxian (Minzhou), Baongan, Lintao (Didao), for many years at Chone and elsewhere along the Amdo-China border. In 1899 Christie made the first serious attempt by a Christian missionary to evangelize the Labrang region, but had to flee from the unreceptive Tibetans.

Christie arrived at Labrang at the beginning of the Tibetan New Year's holiday into a tumult of Labrang monks, townspeople and many thousands of nomads and pilgrims from all ends of Amdo. Christie and his colleague passed out translations of the Christian Bible, and began to lecture the Tibetans. The Tibetans were at first perplexed, then outraged that these foreigners were proselytizing in their midst on one of Tibet's most auspicious festival days. Such attacks on Buddhism were thought to generate evil, especially on the occasion of the community-sponsored festivities and prayers for good luck for the coming year. The Tibetans first threatened the missionaries and destroyed the Gospel literature. The missionaries ignored them. Soon the

Tibetans started to throw dirt and rocks at the missionaries and beat and chase them with increasing ferocity. Christie and his colleague were rescued just in time by the Tibetan militia posted at the monastery. The soldiers took them to the monastery where they were courteously detained and subsequently given the privilege of observing an important Tibetan Buddhist monastic ceremony. However, after the ceremony, the Labrang officials made it clear that these missionaries were not welcome at Labrang, and deported them immediately.[74]

In spite of the resistance of the Tibetans to foreign missionaries and the decades of hostilities between the Hui and the Tibetans, the presence of the CMA mission at Labrang gradually strengthened. By 1919 missionaries were allowed temporarily to rent rooms in Labrang town. The Tibetans' wariness of these foreigners with their all-powerful God continued until Marion and Blanche Griebenow slowly made friends with some Labrang authorities, the Fifth Jamyang Shaypa and many ordinary Tibetans. This is their story.

Blanche Willars and Marion Griebenow were two young Christian missionaries who travelled to Labrang in 1922-1923 and became neighbors and friends of the Alos, Labrang's leading family. They met at Nyack College, New York, were engaged there, and married a few years later in Chone (April 17, 1923), itself an autonomous Tibetan principality[75] a few days by horseback from Labrang Monastery. Like many missionaries before them, they endured considerable hardship, but they managed to establish a Christian missionary base at Labrang that lasted for nearly twenty-eight years. During this time they raised three sons and a daughter and established an extended family of Christian converts.

Marion Grant Griebenow was born on August 30, 1899 in Deer Creek, Ottertail County, Minnesota to August W. and Anna Mumm Griebenow, into a large family with four sisters and a brother. He spent his adolescent years in Minnesota farm country, attending rural schools through his first year of high school and working on his family's 640-acre wheat farm. His parents were devout Christians in the German Evangelical Church, and Marion went to Sunday school regularly, where he studied basic Christian theological and moral principles. August and Anna hoped that young Marion might follow in the footsteps of his maternal grandfather, a preacher in the evangelical tradition.

After an uneventful but normal rural American childhood, Marion's life began to change dramatically. The story goes that after the seventeen-year-old boy attended a Christian revival service given by the Reverend C.C. Brownell of the Christian and Missionary Alliance, his dedication to religious life steadily increased.[76] Church records note that he modified his personal conduct at this juncture, "abstaining from tobacco, alcohol, and foul language." A year later (1917) on a summer evening Griebenow heard the Reverend E.C. Swanson lecture on the Christian theme "He whom the Son makes free is free indeed." The next day while plowing the fields on the family farm the full impact of this "freedom" hit Griebenow. He went down on his knees and pledged his life to God's work, a lifetime career in pastoral work.

In 1917, at a local revivalist meeting, Marion Griebenow met the founder of the Alliance Training Home, later called the St. Paul Bible College and now Crown College. After negotiations, he set out for St. Paul in November 1917 to begin his two sixth-month terms, which he completed over the following two years. He was described as "a country lad of nineteen years who had earned the train fare from his father's farm to the Twin Cities by tending a carload of cattle."[77] Griebenow was a tall, gangly farm boy from Minnesota, dressed in a brand new pair of overalls purchased for the occasion, [who] walked onto the campus of St. Paul Bible College and announced that he had come to study. He knew nothing of the procedures for application and acceptance; he knew only that the Lord had called him and that he had responded. The school waived normal routine and enrolled Marion Griebenow as a student.[78]

In the course of his studies at St. Paul, young Griebenow made contact with Reverend William Christie, one of the first missionaries to attempt serious Christian evangelical work at Labrang, who was visiting the school from his mission post in eastern Tibet. Griebenow was impressed by Reverend Christie, and when the visitor asked his audience who amongst them would dare to take up the cause of the fledgling Christian missions in Tibet, Griebenow resolved that this was his true calling. Christie's requests for missionaries to Tibet were doubtlessly challenging to young Griebenow, who could have had no more than marginal knowledge of that remote mountainous country. Nevertheless, M.G. became fascinated with Tibet, then considered to be the most remote place on earth both geographically and spiritually. He soon resolved to travel to Tibet to spread the Christian message. Later, while in Bible School in St. Paul, Minnesota, and while at Nyack College in New York State, he met other missionaries working in Tibetan regions, which strengthened his commitment to join them in their work.

After completing St. Paul's six-months-per-year, two-year program, Griebenow enrolled at Nyack Missionary Training Institute in September 1919, part of present-day Nyack College, located some forty miles north of New York City. During this time he sought news of Tibet, with little success. While there he met Miss Blanche Willars, a classmate, to whom he was eventually engaged. After finishing his two-year course of study at Nyack, at age twenty-one, Marion Griebenow volunteered for and was appointed to the Tibet mission in May 1921. Shortly thereafter, on 15 September 1921, he left Vancouver, British Columbia, on the Canadian Steamship Lines' *Empress of Asia*, bound for China and Amdo, by way of Shanghai.

On arrival in Shanghai, Marion Griebenow enjoyed a relatively warm reception from the Christian missionaries and their congregations there. He soon left Shanghai by riverboat, voyaging up the Yangtze River to the city now known as Wuhan.[79] During the course of his travels in inner China, Griebenow began to familiarize himself with things Chinese—foods, customs, languages, bartering, and the Chinese world. It is notable that Griebenow and the missionaries assigned to this region of Tibet were not encouraged to learn Chinese, but Tibetan, in the dialect particular to Labrang. After people disembarked from the riverboat in Wuhan, their travel inland became steadily more difficult and rugged.

Blanche Willars was born in Wilmington, Delaware, on July 31, 1897, the youngest of seven children. Their family held membership in the local Methodist Church. Like Griebenow, she attended Christian revivalist meetings conducted by the Christian and Missionary Alliance, and later made the commitment to dedicate her life to Christian mission work. While a student in Wilmington, Blanche worked in church groups and with female inmates in the local jail.

As a young woman, Blanche Willars had deep religious convictions and a strong sense of social responsibility. Not content to stifle her intellectual and creative capabilities in the confines of the sequestered role of the nineteenth-century wife, mother and homeworker, she knew her strengths and took the Christian message seriously. Even at this early stage in her career, Blanche became interested in evangelical missionary work in general and specifically in the Chinese and Tibetan missions.

Blanche met young Griebenow during her studies at Nyack, where she was also moved to volunteer for foreign service. The record states that she made a marital commitment to Griebenow, but there was certainly no guarantee that they would be able to live and work together in the field. Much to the horror of her family and traditional society, Blanche volunteered to travel to remote Tibet, of all places, alone and unescorted at first, and eventually in the company of other women missionaries, and finally as Marion Griebenow's wife, settling at Labrang. It is remarkable that she made her decision independently and followed through on it, even in light of reports of Christian missionaries in Asia being murdered, raped, paraded naked in public, and living in the midst of drought, famine, disease and warfare. Blanche thought it was the best place to go since, being the worst, the need for people like herself was the greatest.

Blanche Willars was clearly an exceptional individual. While service in any foreign mission was extremely difficult, it was even more so in such remote and undeveloped regions as northeastern Tibet. As is well documented, there were few women missionaries and fewer unmarried ones. Their hardships were compounded by the prejudices against women common in the USA in the 1920s, in newly Republican China, in the traditions of tribal and monastic Tibet, and in the eyes of the local Hui. After her graduation from Nyack College in 1921, twenty-four-year-old Blanche travelled across the United States to Vancouver, British Columbia, ignoring repeated requests and warnings from her family members to give up this foolish venture. She remained unmoved by their "disgust with a church or mission board that would send single girls across the Pacific Ocean when they had not been outside the United States before!"[80] Despite all remonstrations, on October 13, 1921, Blanche Willars left Vancouver for Shanghai. The weather was foul and continuing rough seas were predicted.

Like Marion before her, Blanche spent a short time with the missionaries in teeming Shanghai, getting her first images of the beauties and harshness of life in Asia. She proceeded almost immediately up the Yangtze River to Wuhan, where she was lucky enough to meet up with Marion Griebenow before their separate departures en route to Chone, an important Tibetan Buddhist center, first visited by Christian missionaries in 1895 and now a Christian missionary outpost.

After separate overland trips from Wuhan, Blanche and Marion met again in Xian. They then travelled with a party of missionaries to Chone. Life was tough by their standards and sanitary conditions were extremely poor. The diet was different from anything they had known, but food was plentiful for them. As they were travelling late in the year, they endured the bitterly cold Chinese winter. From Xian the small party proceeded by mule-cart over mountains and through streams and rivers, going westward toward the Tibetan highlands, experiencing the many hardships burdening the peoples they passed.

The next major stop on their journey was the ancient walled city of Tian Shui, which at that time was the location of a well-developed Christian mission. From Tian Shui they travelled on through Longxi to Lintao (Didao), the center of all CMA mission work in northwest China and northeast Tibet, their "Kansu-Tibet Border" mission. Travel beyond Lintao (Didao) was much more rugged, and to accommodate this, lady travellers were borne up the mountain paths in palanquin-like litters rigged between two mules. Though precarious to the travellers, this arrangement carried them through the three-day journey over high mountain passes and swift rivers. The entire entourage

Tibetan nomads, a familiar sight at Labrang. Their yak skin garments wrap around in cold weather and fall to the waist on warm days. These fellows wear consecrated amulets for protection against physical and metaphysical dangers.

arrived in Chone on January 13, 1922,[81] at seven o'clock in the evening. Blanche and Marion were assigned to their temporary stations, Marion to the predominantly Tibetan Lintan (Taozhou Old City)[82] near Labrang, and Blanche to Chone. The following Monday morning the men continued on their horses for the three-hour ride to Lintan (Taozhou Old City).

For the next months Blanche in Chone and Marion in Taozhou Old City immersed themselves in the study of the Tibetan language with the available limited resources. They used an unpublished draft translation of the *New Testament in Tibetan* by Reverend Y. Gergan of Lahore, Pakistan,[83] which Marion Griebenow was destined to revise in 1957.

Mission regulations forbade matrimonial alliances between recruits until both were established in-country and fluent in the local languages. The Griebenow Archives record that the latter rule was a powerful factor, promoting remarkable progress in language studies! Thus, while young Griebenow lived on the border of northeast Tibet and China, not far from the still hostile Labrang community, Blanche was required to stay at the Christian mission in Chone, with the Reverend and Mrs. A.J. Hansen.

In addition to all of the other obstacles, the new Tibetan mission projects had no funds. Initial support came from Blanche Willars' home church in Wilmington and subse-

A Tibetan nomad, her hair done in popular style, feeds her baby through an animal horn.

quent funding from a group of ladies in Sheboygan, Wisconsin, who as a group pledged a dollar a day for a year. Later donations from Christian and Missionary Alliance chapters sustained the Griebenow Labrang mission for its duration.

Marion went to Labrang first, in January 1922. During his first short-term visits and later extended residence at Labrang, he travelled around the Tibetan communities in the region, primarily to improve his spoken Tibetan and to familiarize himself with Tibetan customs. He and Blanche reported much Chinese influence mixed with Tibetan lifestyles in the Taozhou Old City and Chone regions.

Marion Griebenow's first letter from Labrang—"Tibet itself," in his own words—is dated March 1, 1922, the eve of a major New Year's festival.[84] Labrang was vibrant with religious and festive energy. His first impressions on this early month-long visit give us an interesting picture of old Tibetan culture. He notes that the monastic community consisted of about five thousand Tibetan monks, led by the Fifth Jamyang Shaypa, a six-year-old reincarnation of the previous head lama. On arrival the visiting missionaries were given a tour of the five main temples, one for each of the traditional five Buddhas. Griebenow wrote of the impressive religious faith of the Tibetan people, who prostrated themselves to the Buddha images so much that "there were deep furrows and holes right in the wood!"[85] He was amazed that Tibetans would prostrate themselves in a slow advance around the circumference of the entire monastery, which he estimated as about two miles. He visited many temples of Buddhist minor deities, and a large assembly hall capable of seating about two thousand.

Griebenow wrote of the strange but satisfying Tibetan diet of meat and [Chinese or Hui style] long fresh boiled noodles; spruce forests with abundant wildlife; large numbers of sheep, horses and yaks used for food, hides, and

A Tibetan nomad couple arrives at Labrang. She rides "like men," wearing a hat typical of the region. Both are dressed in yak skins.

transportation, the latter in place of the carts in common use in China; and the fact that women in Labrang were much more open and equal in status than Chinese women. He noted that they rode horses through town "like men."

The attitudes of Tibetans with respect to women's roles came as something of a revelation to the Griebenows. On several occasions Blanche and Marion noted that "the Tibetan women are much different from the Chinese in that they

A Tibetan prognosticator (sngags pa) *in ritual dress and long hair unravelled, with a disciple.*

are perfectly free, and a Chinese woman may hardly speak to a man."[86] Marion wrote that

> [t]he Tibetan women do not think anything of it in the least to run around naked to the waist all the time if it is warm enough, although they never go any farther than that except for the youngsters who, if it is warm enough, think nothing of running around perfectly nude until the age of eight or ten years. It is quite a shock when a person first comes out here, but it doesn't take long to get accustomed to even that.[87]

On return to Taozhou Old City after his first excursion to Labrang, Griebenow wrote that it seemed "good to get back to civilization of some kind,"[88] attesting to the rugged quality of life in Labrang. However, he also wrote that he would be glad when "We [he and Blanche] could go up to those places and stay for good."[89] This displays the Griebenows' genuine inspiration by and devotion to the Tibetans, so evident throughout their photos and writings. On leaving Labrang for the three-day ride back to Taozhou Old City that first time, he wrote that on their departure in late March 1922, it snowed heavily. From a high pass, they looked back at the mountain range behind Labrang looming up thousands of feet, and beyond that the snowcapped peaks of Tibet across the Tao River, "always called the entrance to central Tibet."[90]

Over the next months Griebenow and his fellow missionaries assigned to the region explored the countryside and settlements of northeastern Tibet, always concentrating on improving their language skills. Griebenow wrote extensively of the region, largely populated by nomads, but with substantial settlements of Tibetans, Mongols, and several monasteries. The missionaries were met with curiosity, fear, and amazement on the part of the Tibetans, many of whom had never seen a foreign face. Griebenow recalls an incident in which their money was considered useless, as it was said to change into stone overnight. They managed to overcome this by letting some Tibetan merchants hold their funds overnight; when the money was still money the next morning, they were able to buy supplies. The young missionaries quickly learned the facts of life in untamed Tibet. There was famine and frequent food shortages on the Sino-Tibetan border in those days, and many local people died of starvation. Extra people were a drain on scarce food supplies.

This woman shows her wealth and tribal style with the elaborate metal and semi-precious stone headdress woven into her hair. The entire family is dressed in yak skin; children often have butter smeared in their hair to insulate against the cold.

A Tibetan falconer.

Fortunately for the missionaries, Marion and his colleagues functioned as doctors. Their foreign demeanor and basic competence in first aid won them much admiration and, with it, the tolerance of the Tibetans. The Labrang region, though part of the Tibetan nation and at least nominally Buddhist, was by no means a heaven of kindly saints or bodhisattvas. Proud nomads and ferocious local bandits guarded their pastures, properties, and territories with a vengeance. Trespassers and travellers were often robbed and sometimes killed. The missionaries treated these facts with respect and carried pistols whenever venturing into unexplored Tibetan territory. Griebenow wrote that "The Tibetans, as a rule, are wild, unruly people."[91]

"Wild" and "unruly," indeed. The Griebenows' own personal safety was often threatened by Tibetan, Hui, and Chinese bandits; they sometimes barely escaped with their lives. Blanche Griebenow reminisces about a much later but typical incident, here a meeting with some rather wild and unruly Muslims:

> We were attacked by thirteen Mohammadans as we travelled over a high mountain not far from Ho-chow. Since we were foreigners, they presumed that we were carrying extra money and threw clods of mud at us. They also beat up Marion and took the baby's clothes. The baby [George Griebenow] realized that something was happening and screamed most all of the time. Once or twice Marion swung around just in time to knock over some of the fellows. He didn't hurt them much, but his action helped him not to be stabbed by their knives. But it was a treacherous time for a few hours. Marion looked bad. He had four big welts across his forehead and was covered with dirt where the clods of mud and dirt hit him. We had a long walk down the mountain because Marion's horse had fled.[92]

In September of 1922 Griebenow spent his first long stay alone in Labrang in preparation for the establishment of the mission there. He passed his days in conversations with the local Tibetans, both lay and monastic, and travelled extensively in the neighboring nomads' districts. Griebenow seemed to enjoy travelling; he wrote of many long trips over high mountain passes in very severe conditions, through forests, high plains, and steep valleys. He saw the abundance of wildlife in old Tibet. He wrote of foxes, rabbits,

This Tibetan nomad shows the traditional dress common to nomad men, women, and children. All often used this as their only garment, normally baring themselves to the waist in the warm sun and bundling up in cold weather. On several occasions the Griebenows wrote that Tibetan women from all segments of society were in general much more free than Chinese women.

and "pheasants galore" and of wild horses and yaks on the high plains nearby. He notes that the Tibetans regarded animal life as sacred; though they lived on a diet based on mutton and yak meat, they never killed for sport, for this was sinful. If the missionaries did so, "it took away [their] influence among the Tibetans."[93]

In the early months at Chone conditions were more difficult for Blanche. Unlike the men, who were allowed to travel freely, all young female missionaries were required to stay inside the compound at Chone. They could stand just outside the gate and invite passing Tibetan or Chinese women in, but under no circumstances were they allowed to speak to men. They were advised that if a man even looked at them, they were to "decorously lower their eyes."[94] Thus, there was no small reaction in the local community when the foreign missionary men from Taozhou Old City, including Griebenow, were allowed to come and visit the ladies and fiancées in Chone. Blanche seemed disappointed that even after several weeks in Chone she and the other women missionaries saw only one red-robed Tibetan walking by their compound, to whom they did not speak.[95] Blanche eventually taught Tibetan children, always remembering to include the Gospels, but unlike Marion she did not go on evangelical outreach "tours." Judging from Marion's and Blanche's records, circumstances at Chone were quite different than those at Labrang, Chone being more conservative in their view, perhaps because of the established mission and the Chinese representative there.

The account of the Griebenow marriage reveals much about life in eastern Tibet. Blanche wrote that

> Finally, the long awaited day arrived! On April 17, 1923 M.G. Griebenow and I were married in a ceremony performed by Reverend Hansen in the Hansens' living room in Choni. Mrs. Hansen, wonderfully kind and thoughtful, arranged everything beautifully. She was mother, big sister, and everything else a girl needs on her wedding day when her own family is ten thousand miles away. I preferred to have the word "obey" omitted from my vows. Also present was the Choni Prince, the highest Tibetan authority in that area, who provided the wedding feast afterwards. The food he served was the very best—many delicious and exotic dishes. It was unforgettable. This Choni Prince was kind to the missionaries, a fact we greatly appreciated, but he never became a Christian even though the missionaries made every effort to win him to the Lord. He continued to live in sin and be extremely cruel to his subjects. He had hundreds of men shot or beheaded and their heads displayed in public places. Finally, his own officers, fearing for their own lives and the lives of their families, brutally murdered him but spared his wives and children.[96]

Nevertheless, Blanche continued,

> the morning after our wedding we left Choni—M.G. on horseback and I in a mule litter—and set out on the four-day journey across mountains and streams to our new home in Labrang, Tibet. Soon we left Chinese influences behind. The houses were different and so were the people, both in features and dress. We likened the Tibetans to our own American Indians. They had bronze-colored skin and high cheek bones. They loved the outdoor life. Their houses and tents had dirt floors. Their horses, cows, yaks, and sheep did not stay in barns or stables but were tethered close to the houses or tents where their owners lived. The Tibetans were full of curiosity about us. As we smiled and said a few words to them in Tibetan, the children almost danced with glee. We found out for a surety that as we showed friendliness to them, they returned friendliness doublefold or more.[97]

Things changed very much for Blanche once she and Griebenow moved across the mostly unmarked but distinct ethnic Tibetan border in Labrang, "Tibet itself," in M.G.'s

Wool stored in preparation for sale and shipment. Wool was perhaps the single most important export from Labrang.

words. The ethnic picture in this region is one of a progressive shift in culture and tradition from east to west. In the east, cultures, languages, and lifestyles were first predominantly Chinese, with some Tibetan influences, then as the terrain grew more rugged, steep, and higher overall, the Tibetan elements began to predominate, until the Tibetan culture, language, and lifestyle were clearly dominant. This line of demarcation ran roughly from north to south, a continuous meeting zone of Tibetan and Chinese cultures.

Blanche Griebenow's writings describe the town and environment of Labrang, nestled in a high valley flanked by steep slopes. She wrote that the extreme winter temperature went to –20° Fahrenheit, and as high as 85° in the three summer months. As the growing season was so short, the major crop was barley. Marion did some experimenting with vegetables, and enjoyed some success introducing potatoes into the local diet. Blanche's writings tell us that they estimated that there were about 15,000 people from different ethnic groups living in the town of Labrang. She notes a large percentage of Hui and Chinese residents in addition to the five thousand monks in the monastery, and a large but transient nomad population. The lay Tibetans in residence were largely farmers and laborers; in contrast the Hui were traders and the Chinese primarily tailors, potters, and artisans in other crafts.

In her reminiscences Blanche gives a strong impression of the pervasiveness of Tibetan Buddhism at Labrang. She describes how all people, lay and monastic, would pray, prostrate, circumambulate, and engage in religious devotion. She describes the Buddhist religion as ubiquitous in Labrang. Blanche was given a Tibetan name, Dechen tso (*bDe can mtsho*).

The Griebenows spent much of their adult lives in eastern Tibet—Marion was twenty-two when he arrived and fifty when he left. The Griebenows' reports and observations are thus reasonably reliable. They wrote about the ethnic diversity of Labrang; it was truly a crossroads of Tibetan, Hui, Chinese and even Mongol and Russian cultures. In the eyes of the Griebenows, twenty-seven-year residents of Labrang, Labrang was part of Tibet. They were excited to establish a mission in what was in their eyes truly "Tibet"; they mention the Tibetan authority at Labrang on numerous occasions. They bought their land from Labrang Monastery, and drew maps marking Tibetan and Chinese boundaries, with Labrang well inside what they, and apparently the Tibetans, considered part of Tibet. There were, however, places where Tibetans lived that were claimed by the Chinese in this region, and vice-versa, places where Chinese lived that were claimed by the Tibetans.

The Hui were close neighbors and active trading partners. The Chinese, pressing in from the east, were a continual force to be reckoned with, and though they traded actively in Labrang's markets, they were, like the Hui, clearly regarded as foreigners by the Labrang Tibetans. Still, the Griebenows recorded many commercial connections with the Chinese heartland. In a late life memoir, George Griebenow, the son born to Marion and Blanche in 1926, noted that

> [t]he Tibetans barter and trade their wool, mutton, butter and cheese for gold, silver, spice, tea, flour and various other commodities from the Chinese. It is a land where there is no wheel. Everybody travels on horseback and they load their goods on the backs of yaks. In order to get into Tibet itself, a person must travel long distances on horseback and on yak. The very narrow trails often go along precipices and cliffs several thousand feet above the valley beneath.[98]

Griebenow wrote about the Tibetans he grew up with, here first commenting on the literacy of a Tibetan monk befriended in Labrang: "He could be a Ph.D. in a university. Highly intelligent, literate, well informed as far as his culture and his way of life is concerned."[99] Other missionaries in the region described the Tibetans as

> [v]ery friendly, very tough people, very strong people, good fighters and very brave and courageous, and [also] very independent. They don't want anything to do with the Moslems to the north, west and east, with the Chinese to the south and east, Mongolians to the northeast and the Russians—White Russians who were expelled from Russia during the Bolshevik

A tile roof covers three large water-driven prayer wheels. The three wooden drums contain thousands of copies of Buddhist prayers. Every time the wheel turns it carries those thousands of prayers to all beings that live in or come into contact with the flowing water.

Revolution and settled as fur traders along the Chinese-Tibetan border—to the northwest. [The Tibetans] are totally isolated, they don't mix with any of them.[100]

George Griebenow gives a remarkable description of old Amdo, full of natural beauty:

The Ceremony Courtyard (ston chos ra). Located next to the Maitreya Temple, this open shrine and courtyard were used as a site for different rituals.

The land is very primitive, very rugged, and very beautiful. It is the land of wild flowers that grow in profusion. The peony, the rhododendron, and many beautiful prairie flowers grow all over the landscape. Most of the mountains are snow-capped the year round. The nomadic Tibetans have large flocks of sheep and yaks. They go up and down the mountains according to the grazing and water benefits that accrue to their animals. One Tibetan family may have several hundred sheep and dozens of yaks. The Tibetan nomads live in clusters of yak-hair tents which are arranged in large circles. The animals are brought into the center of the circles in the night for protection against the ravages of the weather and predators, such as foxes and wolves.[101]

Of Tibetan society:

It was a way of life and an integrated religious and social-economic lifestyle. The religion and social structures unified and protected Tibetan family life, their value system, and what they basically needed to develop equilibrium.[102]

During their stay in Labrang, and especially during the early years, the Griebenows found that the fierce and independent Tibetans were surrounded by formidable enemies, trading partners and military allies, the Chinese in Lanzhou and the Hui in Xining. In Labrang itself the Gansu provincial army from the east had a garrison, whose leaders kept in close contact with Apa Alo, the leader of the Tibetan militia. The Griebenows wrote of impressive meetings of high-ranking Tibetans and Chinese, the Tibetans riding in entourages of hundreds of horsemen in yellow dress, and the Chinese likewise posturing with their many troops.

The Hui populations from the trading centers to the north and east were well represented in Labrang.[103] Blanche wrote of the Hui (here including the original grammar in Mr. Sheng's version):

A high-altitude nomad camp.

There was a numerous [*sic*] Moslem population throughout this Kansu-Tibetan border area. Themselves a minority group with religion and culture different from the Chinese or Tibetans, they were usually friendly and helpful to the missionaries. Many of them were merchants with the best-stocked shops in all of the towns. However, they were formidable fighters and fiercely independent. Periodically they rebelled with such fury that

Two local Tibetans armed with long knives, protected by amulets, and dressed in fine fur hats and strong leather boots.

the very thought of another Moslem uprising struck terror into the hearts of their neighbors.[104]

Blanche also mentioned instances of bloody skirmishes between Tibetans "on robbing expeditions" and Hui traders, and subsequent retaliatory skirmishes. The Chinese had no control over the Hui or the Tibetans, a situation that forced the Griebenows to respect the local authorities.

Every step of the way was an ordeal for the Griebenows; it was no small task getting a foreign mission started. Their first appeal to the CMA for funding for living quarters in Labrang was rejected; their home for the first year, 1923-1924, was in an apartment over a stable, with an open square market area in front. Blanche wrote:

> The rooms which M.G. had arranged for us were on the second floor of a small house on the main street of the town. We wondered if the creaking steps would last until we got our few belongings up there. They did and, surprisingly, though the creaking grew worse, lasted for several years. Our Moslem landlord and his family lived in the other half of the building. The large room below us was occupied at night by three cows and two horses. Because of the cracks between the floor boards of our rooms, we were all too well aware of what was going on downstairs, but we slept quite well in spite of the mooing and neighing! The houses along the street were joined together, and a narrow wooden platform about eighteen inches wide ran along both the front and back of the buildings at second floor level, making an excellent place for our neighbors to walk along and look in to see what the foreigners were doing. We had covered the window frames, which were about two feet square, with white paper stuck on with a flour and water paste, and in the center of each, we had placed a two or three-inch square of glass which we had brought with us, knowing that none would be available there.[105]

Over the following months Blanche and Marion made efforts to become personally acquainted with the Tibetans, visiting neighbors' homes and frequently inviting people to theirs. Marion made many efforts to befriend monks and lamas from the monastery, but with only marginal success. Some Tibetan monastic authorities rejected the Griebenows' evangelism entirely.

In the summer of 1924, the Griebenows were granted CMA funds to build their own home, complete with flowers and vegetables nursed with care from seeds from the USA. The story of their permanent home in Labrang reveals much about the tenor of life in pre-Communist Tibet. The Griebenow home was built almost simultaneously with the Hui siege and war in Labrang, and the flight of the Alo family and their supporters. The Tibetan community was not receptive to foreigners in general, and as we have seen, missionaries with strong anti-Buddhist agendas were most unwelcome, particularly when the threat of Hui hostilities was present. It is thus a credit to the Griebenows' resilience and strength of purpose that they were able to win the approval of the Tibetan lay people and permission to purchase land from the monastic establishment at Labrang. Once the funds were made available, Griebenow had to negotiate with monastery officials, on their terms and in their style. The land-purchase process was extremely long and convoluted, but after many months of requests, negotiations and gifts, the monastery granted the Griebenows permission to purchase a parcel of land for the new mission building.

It is interesting to speculate how the Tibetan monastic authorities evaluated the Griebenows. It is most probable that the authorities at Labrang debated the presence and status of the new religious system in great detail. When

Alak Shabdrung Tshang, the author of the commemorative volume on the Fifth Jamyang Shaypa and, according to the Griebenows, a donor of substantial funds to Labrang Monastery.

Alak Gungtang Tshang, 1934, age 10.

These two nomad women display the inquisitiveness and broad smiles the Griebenows mention in their writings.

Griebenow asked what the lamas would like in return for permission to buy land, they responded quite specifically that in addition to other gifts, they would like to order some items from the United States displayed in the Griebenows' two-year-old Montgomery Ward catalogue! Thus it came to pass that Labrang Monastery came into possession of a brand-new American-made two-burner wood-burning cookstove, several pairs of boots, and an array of various and sundry items from Montgomery Ward in Chicago.

The actual construction of the two-story residence took much planning, importing of special materials, and searching for craftsmen. The Tibetans helped the Griebenows as much as possible; the mission compound was constructed in Tibetan style, and the house to the Griebenows' specifications. For the landscaping, the Griebenows hired over two hundred Tibetan laborers! Finally, the workers covered the walls of the house with blue clay, and later covered it with a "buff-yellow,"[106] which became well-known throughout the entire region.

While at Labrang, Blanche and M.G. Griebenow raised a family of four children. On May 12, 1926, their first son, George William, was born very close to Labrang, in Lanzhou, the capital of Gansu Province. He left Labrang at age fourteen to receive an education in the USA and went on to a multi-faceted career of Christian ministry, heroism in war and local politics. George Griebenow was an active member of his social and economic communities, first in Iowa and then in the Minneapolis area, until his passing on April 20, 1987.

Their second son, Marion Grant Griebenow, Junior, nicknamed "Junior," was born in Labrang in 1931, and left at age nine. He currently teaches health and physical fitness at Jackson Community College in Michigan.

The third son, Paul Verner Griebenow, was born in 1933 in Lanzhou and died in 1935 of dysentery en route to the United States. He was buried in Kobe, Japan.

On June 28, 1939, Blanche gave birth to a daughter, Lois, in Lanzhou, Gansu. Lois lived with the family until age five, when she returned to the USA. She lived in Israel during her parents' posting in Jerusalem, earned a bachelor of science degree from Nyack College in New York, and settled in California.

The oldest son, George, made the strongest bonds with the Tibetan children, and his recollections are an eloquent source for this narrative. He warmly recalls his childhood in the 1930s:

> I enjoyed growing up there and I trusted these kids and they trusted me. There were no cultural or racial [prejudices]. I had all I could do to compete with them on horseback and firing a rifle and getting along with them. The [Tibetan children] were very charming, very lively, full of games, full of fun, full of mischief, very optimistic kids. Beautiful people, they're handsome people, very attractive. They were athletic, acrobatic, they were very good at gymnastics, but above all the Tibetans had a great sense of humor. They loved practical jokes and unless you could give and take in the field of practical jokes and story-telling and narrative, you were not very well accepted. I remember being very well accepted and being able to compete at the level of the Tibetans and they would no more think of me as an invader or person with a Christian religion as any one in their own society. I spoke their language, I dressed like they did, I accepted them and they accepted me. It was a tremendous source of education. After being exposed to so many races, religions, and so many forms of life and having observed first-hand the lifestyles of people some of whom were illiterate, many of the missionary kids saw there was something higher than even formal education.

The Griebenows, ca. 1941. Marion, George, Blanche, Marion Junior, Lois.

Two Tibetan boys—one full of smiles and the other adult dignity—on horseback at Labrang.

I guess as a youngster I would say that the wisdom of the hills and the valleys of Tibet, the land of the panda bear, the land of the snow leopard, the land of beauty and isolation taught me as much as I would ever have to teach them. And the Tibetan people themselves won my open admiration and I did not consider them in any way inferior or superior to myself but as human beings. I was born there, I grew up with them, I saw them have children, I suffered with them, I enjoyed them, entered into their holidays, and [shared] their religious experiences. They lived a very raw and competitive lifestyle against the natural odds, against their Chinese enemies, against their other neighbors, and against the limited resources of the highlands of Tibet.[107]

Marion developed alliances on his many excursions into the surrounding nomad encampments by administering first aid and gradually developing his reputation as a doctor.

Sick people by the scores began arriving at our home asking for 'Uncle Doctor' (*Agu Manpa* in Tibetan). Many ailments responded beautifully to such medicines as aspirin, Epsom salt, or quinine, and hundreds of aching teeth were extracted.[108]

Griebenow started treating more and more people, and in time was travelling back to China for medical supplies and instruction in first aid. Additionally, since he was always praying, and seemed to have some success, he was regarded as something of a shaman, and was given a Tibetan name, Shayrab Tenpel (*Shes rab bstan 'phel*).

Once Griebenow was called on to administer first aid to the patriarch of a group of Tibetan nomads who had been critically wounded in battle with a neighboring group. Though entirely untrained in trauma and triage techniques, Griebenow was able to improvise basic first-aid measures, cleaning the wound, cooling the patient's fever, and keeping him hydrated. This therapy proved effective, and earned him the respect and admiration of these Tibetan nomads for life. When the patient recovered and was preparing a retaliatory strike against the neighboring nomads, he came to the Griebenows on the eve of the attack. He gave his thanks to Griebenow, declared his intent to do battle in the coming days, and asked Griebenow to become his "blood-brother," by drawing and

Nobles and senior Buddhists stayed in this type of tent while travelling.

mixing their blood, binding themselves for life. Additionally, as a consequence of this bond, in the event of the death of the nomad in battle, the nomad told Griebenow, "my wife will become your wife, my parents your parents, and my sheep, oxen, yaks, everything will become yours."[109] Griebenow took this opportunity to deliver a powerful Christian message to the nomad, which deterred him from doing battle and thus precluded the need to take the nomad's wife, parents and livestock. Yet he maintained the close "blood-brother" relationship with this group of nomads for over twenty-five years. Griebenow's daughter Lois [Kemerer] later wrote:

The Tibetans' loyalty, however, was just as intense as their ferocity. After Dad helped a bandit leader back to health after a near-fatal stabbing, the bandit sliced open his own finger and mixed blood with the man who saved his life. Dad was then considered a blood-brother for life. Years later, Dad's party was ambushed by this very bandit pack. He called out the name of his blood brother and the attack was called off.[110]

Many such incidents, and the more routine tooth extractions and first aid, spread the Griebenows' reputations as healers and holy persons throughout northern Amdo. Soon the Griebenow home and mission became a regular stopping place for nomads, and a haven for the sick and curious from all over Amdo. One of their colleagues related that Marion was

> a mountain of a man with a whirlwind of a heart, and has the spirit of a true missionary pioneer. To pray, to plan, to plod, and to succeed sum up his characteristics, and his pleasing personality attracts Tibetans by the scores to the guest hall. Mrs. Griebenow, vivacious and attractive with her dark hair and eyes which

Marion, Marion Junior, and Lois Griebenow, ca. 1941.

delight the Tibetan women, has done much work among the Chinese and Tibetan refugees during the devastating bandit raids of the last few years.[111]

Marion Griebenow went on a mission tour in 1932 and noted that conditions had changed a lot, that "in most places people had lost their suspicion of the foreigner," but still held on to superstitions concerning the extraordinary powers of foreigners.[112] An account written at the Griebenows' mission in 1932, most likely by the Griebenows, gives an interesting description of life in the Labrang community in the early 1930s. The following selection contains a picture of everyday life at Labrang that details the trading patterns of the different groups of Tibetans, Hui, Chinese and other tribal groups.

> Down from the grasslands riding behind slowly moving oxen laden with wool, felts, skins, pelts, leather ropes, butter, and other products such as a pastoral people produce, come the nomads to the flourishing and wealthy center of Labrang, seat of northeast Tibet's most influential monastery. Wearing fox fur or lambskin hats, heavy sheepskin coats girded tightly about the hips with red silk girdles, leather breeches and felt-lined leather boots, they are perhaps the very essence of simplicity. In their girdles they carry the crude, but deadly, swords, and on their backs are slung modern rifles or matchlocks; or if they are too poor to buy these, then they carry the twelve- to eighteen-foot spears which at close range can be so destructive. They have postponed some raiding expeditions in order to visit the sedentary district to trade their products for barley, flour, rice, cloth, cooking utensils, and the many attractive goods offered for sale at the market. Five miles above the monastery of Labrang is the limit of agriculture, and beyond, the warring and robber tribes of the hinterland pitch their camps of black, sprawling tents. To follow the valley in which Labrang is located downstream one passes through clans of sedentary

A Tibetan merchant in Labrang's marketplace, offering items for sale to his clientele, the general Tibetan population.

Tibetans until he comes out into the wider valley which forms the backbone of the thriving and populous district of Hochow. By this route come Muslims and Chinese to exploit some of the trade of Northeast Tibet. Bringing silks, gold-brocaded satins, cotton cloth, cotton and silk thread, cooking utensils, knives, and a hundred and one other commodities, they settle in the trading village adjacent to the monastery, or in the monastery itself, and either barter for or buy outright the nomads' products. These simple folks of the grassy vales and craggy peaks fall an easy prey to the scheming and avaricious sons of Islam and Han. At the market, which is held daily in an open space before the monastery, the butter besmeared nomad, tanned to a dark brown, rubs shoulders with his lighter-skinned agrarian brother. Here in the crowd saunter the monks clad in skirts and scarfs of various shades of red and purple. The merchants spread out their merchandise on low tables and shelves, and each one of them plies his trade in a space of ground no bigger than two square yards. All business is carried on by talking price, that is, by the seller, who asks more than he really wants, and the buyer, who offers less than he cares to give. By gradually coming down in price and adding to the original offer, the two parties arrive at a sum agreeable to both of them, and the transaction is done, although the merchant will declare he has sold below cost, and the buyer bemoans his stupidity for giving too much. In this busy market one rubs shoulders with Russians, Kashmiris, Buriats, Mongolians, Ladakhis and Chinese from most of the provinces north of the Yangtze, and a motley crowd of Muslims and Tibetans from sedentary and pastoral districts scattered over Tibet.[113]

This excerpt shows the diversity amongst the Tibetan peoples, the remarkable mixture of nationalities and tribal groups in Labrang, and the fact that the Labrang Tibetan Buddhist monastery was the focal point of the entire region.

Once the early missionaries established themselves in their bases, for example Marion Griebenow at Labrang, they went "itinerating," in missionary jargon. That is, they went on extended tours throughout the surrounding regions, spreading their Gospel as they travelled.[114] Marion Griebenow and his associates spent much time in the saddle in Amdo and Kham, over high mountain passes, through wide open high plains, and across rivers, always in danger of attack by bandits or territorial nomads, always at the mercy of the elements. The phenomenon is later described:

an effort is being made to reach the unevangelized territory of our allotted field by organizing a special evangelistic band consisting of eight men and a leader. They will devote all of their time in reaching the untouched parts of our field. They will leave their families for periods of six months at a time.[115]

Marion Griebenow went on many such journeys to the western high plains and to the highlands south of Labrang.

In December of 1932 Marion Griebenow and his colleagues went "itinerating" once again.

The shadows were lengthening as our mounted cavalcade made its way across the great Kanchia Plain in Northeast Tibet. We were heading towards a group of black yak-hair tents, sprawled in close proximity on a slope that overlooked the rolling grassland. Cattle and sheep by the thousand could be seen grazing leisurely over the plain as a shepherd pointed out to us the tent of a friend of our guide, with whom we were to spend the night. Approaching the tent, we were warned to keep our distance by the fierce attitude of four Tibetan dogs, but their baying brought forth the wife of the friend, who silenced them with a shout, and then greeted us with smiling face. She invited us to enter the men's side of the tent, and sit around the fireplace on mats. Our hostess was a perfect picture of Tibetan womanhood. Her coal-black hair was hanging in scores of braids and attached to a headdress peculiar to the group. Her dancing brown eyes, perfect teeth, and vivacious demeanor, all spoke eloquently of the characteristics of her race. Her form was bare to the hips. Her only garment was made of sheepskins, the upper half hanging by a girdle from her hips, the lower portion reaching to within one inch of the ground. Her nut-brown skin was weather-beaten from long exposure to sun and wind, and her shoulders bowed from bearing heavy burdens. Her pleasure and appreciation at our visit was a marked contrast to the downcast eyes and retiring demeanor of her Chinese neighbors in Northwest China. The tent was low but

One of the Tibetan nomad families that befriended the Griebnows.

spacious, the side walls being built of carrying-saddles for the oxen and bags of fuel. The long, slanting chute for holding fuel and the fireplace itself divided the tent, separating the quarters for men and women. The fire was fed from argols and sheep-dung, conveniently pushed down the narrowing chute into the stove, and the bright red embers raked out from either side of the fireplace formed a pleasant heating arrangement. Above the fireplace, from front to back, the tent itself was also open, leaving a laced aperture of about eight

Blanche and George, on Blanche's mule-carried carriage, 1932. Blanche and other foreign ladies travelled in these palanquin-type vehicles; Blanche travelled in these from Xian to Chone and Labrang on several occasions.

inches for smoke to escape. Our hostess, chatting gaily, quickly prepared milk tea. She scoured the bowls with sheep dung, the Tibetan "Dutch Cleanser," and then spreading butter and parched barley flour before us, invited us to drink. A large slice of butter was put into each bowl and the tea poured over it. As the butter melted, a beautiful golden glow arose, which was blown aside before sipping the tea. The spontaneous respect and affection manifested by the members of the family gave an air of home to this nomad tent.[116]

This experience is representative of the numerous trips and experiences Marion had while travelling among the Tibetans of Amdo. This account is interesting in that it shows that the Tibetan nomads were first of all happy to live their lives in their traditional ways; they were extremely hospitable to friends and guests, contrary to their attitudes towards their enemies, and their level of respect for humanity and basic human comfort shatters the myths that these Tibetan nomads were "uncivilized barbarians."

Blanche and Marion Griebenow hosted a missionaries' conference at Labrang during the Lunar New Year, 1935. The political atmosphere at Labrang was for the moment relatively stable, and the missionary network was well established in Amdo. It was a festive time at Labrang. On New Year's day, the Tibetans

> ...were coming into town in large numbers; nearly all on horseback and many times two on a horse. Even on the family steed is often seen father or mother with the baby in the bosom of the large sheepskin coat and an older child astride behind the saddle. Nomads come from far and near, women and children riding yaks when horses are insufficient, and always loaded with wool and skins on the backs of the cattle, which are also for sale, as well as flocks of sheep. Sedentary folk from the lower timbered valleys come with loads of grain and crude wooden implements such as tubs, shovels, boxes, churns, and ox saddles, [all items] indispensable to the nomads. Chinese muleteers and merchants arrive days ahead with loads and loads of cereals, cloth, cooking vessels and bowls which they offer for trade on the public market place. All of us in this field have found it difficult to excel the Tibetans

in hospitality. Though their standard of living can not afford the comforts of the western world, yet they offer their best to visiting friends.[117]

The Griebenows left Labrang for their second furlough in October 1935 because of the increasingly difficult political situation and their son Paul Verner's illness. Though the mid-1930s were relatively stable, late 1934 and 1935 brought the threat of a Communist invasion to Gansu and Labrang, so much that Nationalist troops were mobilized in the region, and missionaries were once again forced to evacuate. The Griebenow family returned to the United States, and then went back to Labrang in March of 1937.[118]

Griebenow also enjoyed a strong rapport with educated Tibetans, chief among them the Fifth Jamyang Shaypa, with whom, according to other missionaries, Marion Griebenow discussed Buddhist and Christian topics.[119] Further evidence of the strength of their friendship came in 1937 when Marion Griebenow received an unprecedented invitation from the Fifth Jamyang Shaypa. The highest lama of Labrang invited his close friend to accompany him on a year-long pilgrimage to Lhasa. Griebenow had just returned from furlough, but recognizing the rare opportunity, agreed to accompany the Tibetan leader at least part of the way to Lhasa. He travelled with the entourage for about two months, but turned back before reaching Lhasa. The descriptions of the trip itself provide a rare glimpse into the pageantry of Tibetan religious life, and show how Buddhism was a powerful force in the minds of even the most uneducated Tibetans in the most remote places.

> It was quite an impressive sight to see the thousands of horsemen, priests and laymen, driving loaded oxen and mules and horses. The Jamyang Shaypa himself rode in a sedan chair carried on two magnificent mules which were led by a half dozen runners. His chair was always surrounded by hundreds of horsemen and

Jamyang Shaypa receives offerings and gives blessings in front of his tent while travelling through the Tibetan highlands enroute to Lhasa, 1937. His father looks on as Jamyang Shaypa's brothers escort local guests into the Rinpoche's presence.

preceded by flagbearers. As on the first day, so on every halt of the journey, camp was made early and in good order—two large circles of white tents spread out in a wide valley, with scores of other smaller circles of tents on every side. Each had his own position in the camp, and mine was in Large Circle Number Two, considered quite a place of honor. The other circles of tents were the thousands of Tibetans who took advantage of a large crowd with which to make their pilgrimage to Lhasa, the "Place of the Gods." Our way led upward and across, but always a little higher. Grass was green and abundant, providing plenty of forage for the thousands of animals, and flowers were gorgeous in the many colors and varieties. Wild game (antelope, wapiti, blue mountain sheep, etc.) were frequently seen. The Jamyang Shaypa often invited me to his tent, or to go with him on picnic trips when stopping for a day or two. Then we frequently spoke of the gospel of Christ and Perfect Love.[120]

By November 1939 the CMA had established several missions in the region.

> With the addition this year of another territory to our Kansu-Tibetan Border Mission field, we now find ourselves occupying border towns from Shunhua, the Salar-Moslem center in the extreme north and just over the border in Ch'inghai Province to Sungp'an in the extreme south and well over the border into the Province of Szechuan. Traveling one way one would cover about 400 miles from nearly 36 degrees North Latitude to about 32.5 degrees North Latitude between the lines of 102 and 104 degrees East Longitude. At present the only means of travel along this route, which is a well-beaten caravan trail, is by horseback and takes about fifteen days to accomplish the trip one way.[121]

Griebenow writes about "Pioneering Up South," a local expression for travel south from Labrang to Songpan, which required crossing numerous high mountain passes, and is,

The circle of tents of Jamyang Shaypa and his entourage en route to Lhasa, 1937.

therefore, also "up." He started the trip in November 1939, with a full entourage of Tibetan guides, traders, bodyguards, and merchants.

> Our path led still farther "up South," following the branch of the Yellow River. How desolate from here on! Not a tent, village, or person for days, all the way over the pass and down the Sungp'an valley to within twenty miles of that city! Human skulls and whole skeletons were found everywhere along this apparently deserted trail, and we were told that they were the bones of those who dropped by the wayside when the Chinese Communist army made their famous march from South China through Szechuan to Kansu and back eastward to Shansi. We wondered how many of these, whose bones lay bare, had part in the persecution of Christians and missionaries—those dreadful captures and killings that we all read about a few years ago. Ah, "vengeance is mine, saith the Lord...."

Controlling the earth spirits (sa bdag, gzhi bdag). One manifestation of the diverse Tibetan religious sensibilities. Each person represents his family or clan, and erects a flagpole to control malevolent earth spirits in the interest of the family's well-being.

In Sungp'an the Tibetan nomad finds his method of travel on horseback driving yaks as beasts of burden no longer suitable to continue down the steep gorges in search of tea, food, cloth, and other manufactured articles. So we see these articles being brought in from the south, not on mules' backs as is the case in Labrang, but on the backs of men, some of whom carry over 200 pounds, more than a Tibetan nomad would carry on a yak, and the street is abustle with trade. Wool, sheepskins, and hides are the principal exports brought by the Tibetans and the huge bales of tea are greatly desired by them in return. Foodstuffs are not bought in such large quantities as the prices are higher than in border towns in Kansu.[122]

The return trip from Songpan to Labrang was via "a more direct route" over the mountains, but proved to be a harrowing adventure on steep icy cliffs through raging storms.

The next day we crossed a high pass and dropped down into a thick pine and spruce forest, the largest we had ever seen in China or Tibet. We had difficulty finding a clearing large enough to pitch our tents....

That night it snowed hard (we were now once again at a high altitude) and the next morning we had to climb up a high mountain that took us hours. It was very steep and hard on the horses. At the top there were two small forts and a Tibetan *Labtze* (bundle of huge arrows set up for the mountain god). Everything was covered with frost and old snow as well as last night's fresh snow [which] lay many feet thick....

About halfway down we were again in thick woods and the snow was melting so we slid in the mud and slush (it was too steep to ride) to the foot of the hill where a cup of tea quickly made over an open fire tasted good with a bowl of *tsamba* (Tibetan parched barley flour)....

A wealthy Tibetan lady poses on a carpet in a long-sleeved Tibetan robe and fur hat.

We thought we had come over some bad road already, but the worst was yet to come. Everything was rock and steep cliffs. The river, now a large stream down in the main valley, churned and boiled as if in a frenzy to get down the deep trough it had cut for itself into the solid rock. The trail led us either clambering high up over the narrow spurs or creeping slowly along a narrow ledge where one mis-step would have meant disaster in the green torrent below.[123]

Griebenow's trip to Songpan and back to Labrang covered about 700 miles, taking forty-five days.

It is remarkable that even in 1940 the turbulence in China and the world had little effect on Labrang. Blanche wrote "We thank the Lord that in spite of warfare and evacuations of mission stations throughout China, we have had unusual quietness and freedom from political disturbances."[124] In 1941 Marion Griebenow made yet another trip to the south, to Songpan, through the rugged mountains. The story is much the same as those of his other trips; the weather was unforgiving, the scenery beautiful, the bandits threatening, and yet the nomads and old friends remarkably open-hearted and most hospitable.[125] The Griebenows were well aware of the wars in China, and were often forced to travel around battlefields and dangerous areas, fleeing bombings and major military conflicts.[126] The following war years brought further chaos and bloodshed to China and Amdo, but the Labrang region managed to remain relatively secure. However, the situation was deteriorating rapidly, and more and more missionaries were being evacuated from Chinese stations.

In 1945 the Griebenows made their last furlough to the United States, returning to Labrang for their last extended stay in July of 1947. Things had changed considerably. They now travelled by air, jeep, and finally mule to Labrang in a fraction of the time it took in previous years. On this return

they were met by Apa Alo, who told the Griebenows of the death of Jamyang Shaypa (April 14, 1947), his brother. One of Jamyang Shaypa's obituaries, written by Marion Griebenow, was published in the journal of the Christian and Missionary Alliance.[127] These were trying times for the Griebenows emotionally and politically; their written accounts include hopes and prayers for reconciliation between the Tibetans and Chinese, since hostilities at the time were so fierce.[128] This attests to the unfortunate reality that the alliances made by the Labrang Tibetans with the warring Chinese parties, openly participating in Nationalist congresses and covertly assisting the Communists, became weaker and dissolved in these years.

The Griebenows carried on with their work even in the midst of political chaos. Nomads still came to visit their home and exhibited characteristic Tibetan opinions:

When [the visiting nomads] were invited into the guest rooms provided for them, they asked permission to stay on the ground in the yard as they would be much more at home there with their tents and heavy furs. "After all, the house just might fall down," they said.[129]

It is remarkable that even in 1947 Marion Griebenow did not hesitate at all to "itinerate" among the Tibetans. Warfare, bandits, and harsh travelling conditions were of as little concern to him in 1947 as they were in 1922.[130] The Griebenows persisted in their work in Labrang, though without the close relationship to Jamyang Shaypa.[131]

By 1949 the situation in China had deteriorated severely. The Communists were still fighting, and the Hui in Gansu still resisting. Bandits were still terrorizing the countryside, and the situation in Labrang was uncertain. Marion Griebenow wrote:

It is a somewhat hazardous trip as there are robbers on the road now and, of course, we have to go by

A volume of the Buddhist Perfection of Wisdom (Prajñāpāramitā) scriptures prepared for public display.

horseback, staying in the open a few nights. The political situation in China is still [volatile but] we are quite peaceful on this field [in Labrang]. If the Communists should take Sian, it would make our position more hazardous. In the meantime the Moslems to the north of us are making feverish preparations for a last stand against the Communists.[132]

These years brought more political changes and shifting alliances between the Tibetans, Muslims, and Chinese.

Blanche and Marion spent most of 1922-1949 in the Labrang region. However, like others in foreign service, they were allowed several visits to their homes in the USA. In sum, they stayed at Labrang for four terms of service, returning to the United States three times. Their first stay at Labrang was for five and one-half years (January 2, 1922-June 9, 1927), then seven years (October 1928-October 9, 1935), then eight and one-half years (March 6, 1937-October 11, 1945), and finally two years (June 27, 1947-August 7, 1949).

The Griebenows fled from the advancing Communist armies on August 7, 1949, never to return. The mission became part of a lost past, no longer a physical presence, but living on in the distant memories of older generations of people in Labrang and in the Tibetan refugee communities worldwide, and through photographic, written, and oral archives collected by the Griebenows. The end of the mission did not, however, end the Griebenow's involvement with Tibetans. Though M.G. and Blanche Griebenow were re-assigned to Jerusalem from 1950 to 1957, and later to Hong Kong and Taiwan from 1959 to 1966, they never gave up their attempts to be reunited with the Tibetans. Their many requests to the Indian government for extended-stay visas among the Tibetans in exile were continually denied, so that M.G. Griebenow was to visit Tibetans again only briefly on one occasion in 1956.

The Griebenows' success at Labrang may be seen first and foremost in the fact that they managed to survive and carry on with their work. The war environment, the complex political situation, and the well-established religious institution that served as a regional focal point together presented daunting challenges to their mission. In their favor they had a combination of diplomatic liaisons, local political connections and a good attitude toward the Tibetans. The Griebenows insisted that fellow missionaries regard the Tibetans with respect. Both Blanche and Marion were often requested to give talks on their approach to dealing with the Tibetan people, speaking on such topics as Marion's "Tibetan Etiquette and Its Bearing on Our Contact with Tibetans for Christ," and Blanche's on "The Best Methods to Direct Evangelization Among Tibetans."[133] Still, the Griebenows did not establish any institutions that survived after their departure. The Labrang region unfortunately became one of the most fierce battlegrounds between the Tibetans, Hui and Chinese. Members of the small Christian community the Griebenows managed to create were either killed or scattered to China, eastern and central Tibet, or into exile.

Marion Grant Griebenow retired in 1966, but remained active in church work in Iowa, Michigan, and Pennsylvania, always keeping his religious goals and his commitment to the Tibetans alive. He died in Cedar Falls, Iowa, on September 30, 1972. Blanche Willars Griebenow spent her final days in Jackson, Michigan, where she died on September 15, 1985. Their work at Labrang, though yielding only a small number of converts, somewhere between one hundred and one hundred and fifty Tibetans and Chinese, and none from the Muslim faith, was nonetheless a remarkable effort. They faced almost unsurmountable odds, but never gave up their determination to win the hearts and minds of the Tibetan people. This book bears witness to their successes, and records the irony and beauty of the Tibetan people's success in winning the Griebenows' hearts and minds.

IV.

LOCAL LEADERS:

THE ALOS—A RELIGIOUS AND SECULAR FIRST FAMILY

Family relations have always played important roles in Asian cultures, and Labrang is no exception. When the Griebenows arrived in Labrang, they were met by members of the influential Alo family, whom they befriended.[134] The prominent role of the Alo family at Labrang is recorded in the Griebenow Archive.

The Alos' story begins in Litang, Sichuan Province, a community on the border of China and eastern Tibet. There was considerable Chinese influence at Litang in the early twentieth century, and Gonpo Dondrup, the patriarch of the Alo clan, negotiated a position for himself in the regional Chinese bureaucracy. His roots were in a Tibetan farming village near Litang called Tsema, a Buddhist community on the border of ethnic China and Tibet. He eventually got a job as minor office manager in the Chinese military bureaucracy at Litang, and in 1906 became a local official administrator (a "magistrate," *bao zheng, qu zhang*) under the Qing Dynasty by his association with the notorious Chinese commander Zhao Erfeng. He held this appointment until 1911 when he and his family were forced out of Litang by invading Republicans.[135] He and his family fled from their two-story, ten-room house in Litang. They abandoned their substantial herds and flocks, the income from the Chinese for Gonpo Dondrup's services as magistrate, the annual tax

paid to the magistrate by the local community, and tuition-free schooling for their children.

While in Litang and working for the Chinese Gonpo Dondrup nurtured his Tibetan Buddhist roots by close connection to his younger brother, Nawang Tendhar. Nawang Tendhar played a role in the lives of the Alo family while at Litang. He entered Gewa Tashi Monastery near Litang as a novice, then went to Ganden Monastery in central Tibet where he was granted a Geshe degree ("Doctor of Buddhist Philosophy"). He returned to Gewa Tashi Monastery, where he eventually became Abbot. Thus, the primary authority figures in the lives of the Alo family were Gonpo Dondrup, the patriarch, who worked for the Chinese, and Nawang Tendhar, a highly educated Buddhist monk. The important point here is that in later years the family, including Nawang Tendhar, brought this combination of roles and abilities to Labrang, where they maintained their Tibetan Buddhist identity and at the same time worked with their Chinese neighbors.

Prior to their arrival in Labrang, however, the fortunes of the family changed considerably. Gonpo Dondrup's relationship to the Chinese proved of little use between 1911 and 1919. In those years the family lived as nomads in the Tibetan highlands, where the family grew, and the Alo

The Alo family, ca. 1932. Top row, left to right: Guru Lhatso ('Gur ru lha mtsho), Gonpo Dondrup's first wife; Gonpo Dondrup; Balmang Tsang; Apa Alo;
Jamyang Shaypa; Nawang Donden, Gonpo Dondrup's older brother; Khyenrab Dondrup, Apa Alo's younger brother, son of Gonpo Dondrup's second wife;
bottom row, left to right: a nurse; Tsering Palkyi, Apa Alo's daughter; Amgon, Apa Alo's son; Nawang Gyatso, Apa Alo's younger brother.

children, especially Apa Alo, learned archery, marksmanship, and riding. While in the grasslands, the family maintained their connection to Tibetan Buddhism, and in 1916 they discovered that there was a reborn Tibetan lama in their midst, the Fifth Jamyang Shaypa. In 1919 they escorted the young incarnation into Labrang.

In sum, the Alos were at once tough nomads, Tibetan Buddhists, and familiar with Tibetan and Chinese lifestyles.

They had a reincarnate lama in their midst, and when they entered Labrang it was under siege by neighboring armies, surrounded by regional civil wars and the target of Christian missionaries. While it may be incorrect to represent the Alos as self-sacrificing Tibetan patriots, it is also inaccurate to represent them as a conniving elite. They were sensitive to both humble and aristocratic Tibetans, and to Tibetan Buddhists. They knew how to negotiate with the Chinese, and how to stand up to hostile neighbors. This combination brought them considerable success at Labrang; anything less would have resulted in failure.

Gonpo Dondrup had a large family, raising seven (or six[136]) children with two wives, Guru Lhatso and Nangchi Wangmo. Several of the children were important figures at Labrang; all of them appear in the Griebenow Archive photographs. All were privileged; the children of one mother were apparently not favored over the children of the other.[137]

The eldest Alo son, who became the most important military commander and political figure at Labrang, was Losang Tsewang (b. March 1903), known to his community as Apa Alo, to his intimate family as Zicai, and to the Chinese as Huang Zhengqing. When the Griebenows arrived in Labrang in 1921 and 1922, Apa Alo was about eighteen years old. As a child Apa Alo learned some Chinese school etiquette and enjoyed the benefits of his father's access to Chinese officials. He brought this awareness and his knowledge of nomad lifestyles to Labrang. He eventually rose to be the chief government official at Labrang, endorsed as such by his brother the Fifth Jamyang Shaypa, the religious authority, and later by the Chinese authorities in Lanzhou, who gave him the title of Huang Siling, approximately "Commander Huang." This title signaled Labrang's military alliance with the Chinese in Lanzhou.

Khyenrab Dondrup, Apa Alo's younger brother.

The boyhood and life of Jamyang Shaypa were entirely different from those of Apa Alo, his older brother. He was enthroned at age five, and from then entered a rigorous monastic education that was to continue through his life. The young monk's life was privileged but strictly regimented by his studies in epistemology, logic, ethics, grammar, debate, and a daunting array of precise ritual practices.

Several of their siblings made important contributions to the family's rise to power and to Labrang's struggles. Khyenrab Dondrup (1909-1945), known in Chinese as Huang Zhengben, was six years younger than Apa Alo. An official at Labrang, he became ill and died in 1945 at age 36. Nawang Gyatso (1911-1939), also known as Huang Zhengji, was the leader of the Labrang delegation to the front lines of the anti-Japanese Chinese troops in the cold winter of 1938. He returned ill in 1939 and died at age 28. While these two members of the family were active in politics, their brother Jigme Tsultrim Namgyal (Huang Zhengming in Chinese),

Balmang Tsang; Khyenrab Dondrup; Amgon.

also known as Lama Balmang Tsang (*dBal mang tshang*) was identified as a rebirth of Balmang Choktrul Rinpoche.[138]

Gonpo Dondrup's first daughter, born in 1916, was Adrol. She married the leader of the Khang Panchen Goloks, a subgroup of the Khangsar Goloks. The second daughter, Asur, eventually married the leader of the Khang Kemin Goloks, subgroup of the Khangan Goloks.[139] The marriages of these two daughters served to ally the Goloks with the Labrang authorities.

In the next generation, Apa Alo's son Kalsang Dondrup, or Amgon (Huang Wenyuan), married Tashi Tsering, the daughter of the Mongolian Prince Kunga Paljor, in 1941, and died in 1957. This marriage solved the problem of the lack of a male heir for the regional Mongol leadership. While it is true that Mongol power had waned considerably, it is notable that Amgon, like his siblings, acted for the well-being of the family and the community.

All of Gonpo Dondrup's children and grandchildren helped establish the reputation and influence of the family. His second and third sons were identified as preeminent reincarnate religious leaders and his daughters married important Tibetan territorial leaders. Another son contracted a fatal illness, sacrificing his life while serving as an envoy to Chinese troops at the front in the anti-Japanese War. His grandson married a Mongol princess in another manifestation of solidarity with the Mongols. The rest of his children and grandchildren had distinguished religious and political careers, enhancing the regional status of the family and promoting its interests in dealings with their Chinese neighbors. The impact of the career and life choices of the Alo children should not be underestimated. Apa Alo commanded respect in the eyes of the Chinese and Muslim political and military structures, the two incarnate lamas were emanations of the Buddha in the Tibetan Buddhists'

Wedding photo, 1941. Apa Alo's son Amgon (d. 1957) and the Mongol Princess Tashi Tsering (ca. 1918-1966).

An interesting point of contact between the Tibetan Alos and their Chinese neighbors was the Alos' self-conscious use of Chinese names. In addition to speaking Chinese to their neighbors, the Alos' use of Chinese names for themselves helped make them familiar to the Chinese, reinforcing diplomatic ties, military alliances, and at least superficial cultural resonance.[140]

The Alos took a Chinese surname in the first decade of the twentieth century, before the fall of the Chinese Qing Dynasty and during the reign of the Thirteenth Dalai Lama. When Gonpo Dondrup started his job as a petty official under Zhao Erfeng, the Chinese referred to him as "Hang" (as in Hangzhou city). This "Hang" was still only an approximation of a Tibetan family name, artificial and unfamiliar to the Chinese. Gonpo Dondrup had to be called something that the Chinese could relate to in terms of their subjective and bureaucratic structures. To solve the problem the family adopted the traditional and very popular Chinese surname (*yi bai xing ming*) "Huang."[141] The Chinese name has stayed with the Tibetan family in a remarkable display of intercultural, interregional, and political diplomacy.

The evidence of the continuing diplomacy between the Alo family as the official Chinese "Huang" family and as the powerful nomad Tibetan leaders, the "Alo" family, occurs throughout the history of early twentieth-century Labrang. The Griebenow Archive contains numerous photographs of Apa Alo in traditional Tibetan militia dress, in formal Tibetan court dress, in Chinese military uniform, and elsewhere in a Western-style suit jacket, tie and slacks, with his sons likewise and his wife and daughter in skirts and blouses.[142] This attests to the Alos' skill in diplomacy; their residences at Labrang, their primary language, culture, and religion attest to their identity and commitment to their homes and people. In the midst of this outreaching,

view, and the other children became monastic officials, members of Tibetan and Mongol ruling elites, and political envoys. In sum, the Alo family had considerable military, political, ethnic, and religious power.

negotiating sentiment, there was also a strong recognition of being Tibetan nationals first and foremost and, especially in light of a perceived threat, to assert themselves with determination.[143]

Conversely, in an interesting compromise that lends proof to the prominence of Tibetan culture at Labrang,

> ...both Muslims and Chinese adapted themselves to Tibetan ways in order to deal with them on their own ground. The resilience of Tibetan culture in the face of two self-confident opponents lies in the geography and climate of the frontier as much as in the ethnic identity or religious doctrine. Neither Han nor Hui could exploit the Tibetan highlands as well as the Tibetans did, nor could they fight across them as effectively.... Their economic, political, and cultural contributions to the life of the border area should not be underestimated.[144]

The phenomenon of a "middle ground" in an inner Asian manifestation does seem to describe the situation at Labrang. It is, however, also true that Tibetan was the predominant ethnicity.

The identity of each of these groups necessitated the formation of different working relationships, since each was coming from a different religious and political environment and thus had to redefine itself in order to expedite trade and political discourse.[145] The Muslim groups brought a strong but by no means uniform monotheistic religion to Qinghai and Gansu. The Arabic language came with these religious beliefs, but Chinese was soon adopted and the Arabic language used only for religious purposes.[146] The Hui often "found their best interests served by an alliance with the state or with non-Muslim neighbors against some of their coreligionists."[147] There can be little doubt that the process of religious mixing, or at least religious imitation, took place.[148]

The Chinese came to Labrang laden with manufactured goods, their images of empire, and a complex of Confucian, Daoist, and Buddhist practices. The Chinese, like the Hui, were forced to conform to Tibetan standards in order to acquire Tibetan wool and hides, and to maintain the fragile peace along their borders. The Griebenows came to Labrang with their mission and were accepted in a similar fashion. In return the Griebenows spoke Tibetan, often dressed like Tibetans and made efforts to understand Tibetan culture. Moreover, Gonpo Dondrup, his wives, Apa Alo, Jamyang Shaypa, and their other brothers and sisters lived in proximity to the Griebenows and their four children. The events and details of these two families' lives and the striking differences of experience that the record notes provide a useful tool for understanding the border culture at Labrang.

V.

LABRANG UNDER ATTACK:

CIVIL WAR AND REVOLUTION, 1922-1949

L abrang is at the crossroads of several cultures. Its location has served the community well but has sometimes made it vulnerable to outside attack. It is important to be aware of what was happening throughout the region during the first half of the twentieth century, since the events in the neighboring regions certainly had an impact on Labrang.

It is no secret that during this period China was in the midst of enormous political, economic and social changes. The entire culture was redefined in the early twentieth century, often painfully, with injustices inflicted by both Chinese and foreign powers. China reasserted its national identity only after much sacrifice and suffering. Meanwhile, the ordeals of the Muslims living in China were also excruciating. These people endured brutality and hardships that are nearly indescribable. One product of the Chinese and Muslim conflicts was a sense of mistrust and animosity that persisted through the first half of the twentieth century. Further, at the same time and from another quarter, the Mongol peoples continued to lose their cultural cohesion both in the Gansu region and in their homelands.

The relevance of these conflicts and changes to Labrang is still not entirely well-studied; this book is only a beginning. I have mentioned the role of the Chinese, Muslims, and Mongols briefly above, but it is still worth emphasizing that Chinese control of Gansu, and Labrang in particular, was in this period intermittent and nominal at best. Similarly, while Hui forces—like those of the Chinese—were always close by, their control of the Labrang region was short-lived and always in dispute. A further complication that must be kept in mind is the precise nature of the relationship between the Chinese and Hui forces. Even though Chinese and Muslim animosity was deep-rooted, the Qinghai Hui forces were recognized functionaries of the early twentieth-century Chinese government. Moreover, with regard to the Tibetans, Apa Alo himself was also a recognized military official in the Chinese system. The crucial factors here are to understand the extent to which these relationships were honored, for how long, and under what conditions. That is, the Hui-Chinese alliance was selectively invoked and enforced. Similarly, the Labrang Tibetan and Chinese alliances were intermittent and hard to enforce. These types of problems were symptomatic of the times throughout the entire region; there was little consistency or dependability in political and military alliances. This made self-sufficiency a requirement for survival regardless of historical events, regional autonomy, or claims of sovereignty. The people at Labrang survived by clever negotiations with their neighbors and by the necessary marshalling of their national resources.

In this short chapter I will not explore the complexities of Hui and Chinese history and their perspectives on each other and Labrang. Here I will only present a brief account of events from the Labrang Tibetans' perspective. This version of the events of the early twentieth century in the contexts of Chinese, Hui, Mongol—and Tibetan—histories is the subject of a much more detailed study.

The beginning of the twentieth century found Labrang Monastery under the authority of the Fourth Jamyang Shaypa (1856-1916). Meanwhile, relations between the Qing Dynasty and the Labrang Tibetans were generally stable during his tenure and thereafter, from the 1870s to the 1920s. Unlike Lhasa or Xining, no imperial resident (*amban*) was appointed by the Qing court to Labrang, and there was no "local administrator" (*tusi*) at Labrang, as there was in Chone. Relations with the Labrang Mongols remained stable, with only a gradual waning of Mongol political authority and a weakening of local Mongol ethnic identity. The local Mongols had largely assimilated Tibetan beliefs and lifestyles by the twentieth century.

The Fourth Jamyang Shaypa was from Kham, Labrang-educated, and engaged in further studies in Lhasa. Labrang was fortunate to have an educated and politically activist leader in the late 1800s and early 1900s; he was a dynamic individual who did much for Labrang Monastery. He solicited donations to construct new buildings at Labrang, developed foreign diplomacy, and negotiated with the Qinghai government to promote continued peaceful coexistence.

The Fourth Jamyang Shaypa did his utmost to prepare Labrang for the turmoil of the twentieth century. Despite his best efforts the four-year interregnum after his death, from 1916-1920, was marked by power struggles between Tibetan officials, notably between factions led by the designated Regent Balmang Tsang, the monastery Manager Li Zongzhe, and the Muslim leader in Xining, Ma Qi.

The Muslims were a powerful force at Linxia/Hezhou in the east and in Qinghai to the west, unafraid of the Chinese. "From 1911 onward, every outside commander in Gansu had to share at least some measure of power with the [Qinghai-based] Ma warlords."[149] The diversity of regional languages, different Muslim sectarian affiliations, lack of food in famine years and territorial boundary disputes often led to conflict, such as the continuous hostilities between the Salar[150] and the Hui Muslims, and between the Muslims and the Chinese or Tibetans. The Qing Dynasty is particularly notorious for its poor treatment of the Muslims in Qinghai, Gansu, and elsewhere in the region.[151]

Throughout the first half of the twentieth century, the basic political problem in the region was the establishment of territorial boundaries, no small task in an area inhabited by diverse tribal groups with many large nomadic populations, civil war and natural disasters—hail, floods, drought, famine, landslides, and earthquakes. Paradoxically, awe, fear, hatred, respect, and cooperation characterized relationships among Tibetans, Mongols, Muslims, and Chinese.

In 1895, the year William Christie went to Labrang, the Muslims attacked and were defeated by the Chinese in Linxia/Hezhou. Chinese government reprisals for the failed Muslim rebellion further sharpened hostilities between all groups of ethnic Muslims and the Han Chinese. Over the next half-century there was a nearly constant series of regional battles. Preemptive and retaliatory attacks on nomadic and sedentary communities were commonplace and often involved the slaughter of women, children, and the aged. These attacks heightened feelings of resentment and hatred which were passed on through generations. Many of the fighters were roving, independent, privately funded bandit armies, motivated to kill only by the promise of

Another of the nomad families who became frequent visitors to the Griebenow household.

plunder, without regard to race, creed, gender, age, or national origin.[152]

The Chinese authorities, recognizing the intractability of the Qinghai and Gansu Muslims, cleverly enlisted them as allies in 1898. The Hui had the reputation of being good fighters and became feared in China. In 1911, after the onset of the Chinese revolution and after over a decade of fighting Chinese battles, the Hui gradually returned to

Qinghai and Gansu. In their homelands they found no Hui government or polity to which they could give their support.[153] Famine and disease were widespread, and refugees clung to life after vicious and repeated attacks by militias and independent bandits from all quarters. Domestic animals died of starvation and crops were left unharvested. In summary, the Chinese revolution in 1911 marked the beginning of a period of chaos and bloodshed in Gansu and in China that lasted until the modern era.[154]

Yuan Shikai, president of the new republic from 1912 until his death in 1916, was remarkably ineffective in his efforts to develop a unified Chinese nation. After his death the strength of provincial military powers increased—there were hundreds of warlords—while that of the central government eroded. China was moving into a state of political anarchy.[155] As one historian has written,

> [t]he warlords fought literally dozens and dozens of wars against one another. They brought terrible suffering to the Chinese people. The most conspicuous feature of warlord politics was the extraordinary rapidity of and frequency with which national and provincial posts changed hands. The warlord period exemplified the extremity of China's territorial disintegration.[156]

Apa Alo may well be considered a regional warlord, albeit one whose aspirations were confined to Labrang and its territories, far removed from the main areas of concern in central China. Yet Apa Alo's hold on Labrang was buttressed by religious legitimacy and was far more lasting than that of most other warlords.

Bandits added to the insecurity of life in Amdo and northwest China. In 1914 the infamous Chinese Henanese bandits called the White Wolves committed atrocities even worse than those of the regional warlords. They were a private army of roving marauders with seemingly insatiable appetites for robbery, murder, rape, and destruction, a large and more ferocious version of similar local groups. The White Wolves marched some 20,000 strong to Gansu but were eventually turned back by the provincial forces and the rugged terrain at Minxian. Still, though they did not reach Labrang, the White Wolves attacked, burned and murdered everyone in Lintan (Taozhou Old City). According to W. Christie:

> On the twenty-fifth of May [1914] T'aochow Old City was taken by storm, and the Wolves immediately set themselves deliberately to destroy every living being within its walls, not only the men and women, the cattle and horses, but down to the very dogs and cats in the lanes. The gates were stacked up to their arches with carrion, and the streets a chaos of corpses.[157]

The Wolves temporarily distracted the Ma warlords from facing the increased Chinese military power in Lanzhou, ordered by Yuan Shikai in 1913. However, after the Wolves were driven off, the new national military threat and the constant depredations of bandits brought the old conflicts to the surface in 1915.

The Fourth Jamyang Shaypa died in 1916, giving the Hui at Labrang and the Salars in Xunhua opportunities to expand their territory. The Henan Prince, the highest ranking Mongol nobleman in Amdo, married to Lukho, a Tibetan, was powerless to intervene. Li Zongzhe, the monastery Manager, either had an illicit affair with or insulted Lukho and subsequently fled to Xining, where he attempted to make an alliance with Ma Qi, a ruthless Hui general. Balmang Tsang became Regent of the monastery,[158] but lacked realistic secular authority. Li Zongzhe remained day-to-day manager and used his position to foment dissent by his constant attempts to gain power.[159] The Qinghai-based

Balmang Tsang and the Fifth Jamyang Shaypa, the two incarnate Buddhist teachers from the Alo family, ca. 1935.

Ninghai Army and the Xunhua Salar forces took advantage of the chaotic climate at Labrang, attacking in November 1918. The Regent Balmang Tsang, unable to raise a significant, well-equipped army, was defeated and Ma Qi established a garrison at Labrang. The Qinghai forces overran the Labrang Tibetans, remaining a constant aggressor in the region and the Labrang Tibetans' main opponent for nearly a decade.

Meanwhile, never far from this chaos, and often in the center of it, the Alo family members did their best to survive by making alliances with their Chinese neighbors, though their neighbors were not particularly well-disposed and even were hostile toward the Labrang Tibetans. Nevertheless, Gonpo Dondrup and Apa Alo continued to cultivate their contacts with the Chinese, building on their relationship established years earlier in Litang.[160]

When the Alos arrived at Labrang in 1919 they were invited to Xining to negotiate the future of the Hui-Tibetan relationship. The event was conducted in regal style, but Ma Qi rejected the Tibetans' demands, chief among which were the removal of the army garrison at Labrang and noninterference in Tibetan affairs.

A missionary's report of a 1921 battle between a group of Amdo Tibetans and the Hui cavalry (less than a year before Marion Griebenow's arrival in 1922) illustrates the explosive hatred between the region's tribal groups. Note that the Christian missionary writer, A.J. Fesmire, sympathizes with the Muslims against the Golok Tibetans, who were later under the jurisdiction of Labrang Monastery. The monastery eventually turned into a support center for these very missionaries and guaranteed safe passage and protection by the Goloks.

During the summer months of the year 1921 God again used the Mohammedans of Western Kansu Province to answer more fully the prayers of His people for the last half a century for the dark land of Tibet. In the month of April an expedition was launched by them, against the wild Goloks, [who are] occupying a large territory five or six days to the west and south-west of the field we are at present endeavoring to occupy. One of the chief natural reasons for the incursion was the killing, by the Goloks, of several soldiers carrying official dispatches and seizing four or five thousand yaks belonging to the High Commissioner. The Goloks consisted of three groups and were a most haughty people, considering themselves impregnable, since they had never been subdued by the Chinese in all their history. But the Mohammedans with their up-to-date firearms practically annihilated one group, and the other two hastened to capitulate. It is reported, though, that the first and most crushing blow was struck through treachery. The three groups were called together to tender their submission. The Goloks were suddenly attacked, and a large number of them were killed. The remainder fled without making any attempt in their weakened condition to avenge their fallen friends. Then followed a chapter of awful bloodshed and cruelty. Men, women, and children were ruthlessly put to the sword and thousands were driven into the Yellow River to perish in its muddy water. A heavy indemnity was exacted, thousands of sheep, yaks and horses driven away, and tons of wool confiscated. Thus is made safe for travel and missionary work a vast piece of country inhabited by thousands of nomads. We are praising God for the advance step He has enabled us to take.[161]

The irony here is that the very Tibetan Goloks whom God and the Muslim forces were fighting later became protectors of the missionaries. At the same time as this fighting was going on Griebenow wrote that in spite of the murderous environment, "I am enjoying it immensely out here in Kansu and Tibet. I wouldn't be in any other field."[162]

The Alos sought allies among the seventy-six militias of the Tibetan tribes in Amdo[163] and attacked the Hui at Labrang in 1922. In 1923 they burned their barracks down. The Hui forces responded in 1924 by showing up with five hundred mounted troops and a list of demands, including more Hui control and higher taxes on Tibetans.[164] Immediately thereafter the Hui forces defeated the Tibetans again, and made conditions at Labrang even more harsh. The record states that many Tibetans were killed and thirty-four buildings burned. The Tibetans had, however, learned their lesson. They made more alliances with more armies, including one led by a regional Chinese general, but since the Chinese were themselves reluctant to confront the Hui fighters, the situation remained unchanged. In 1925 the Hui, Chinese, and Tibetans had a meeting in Lanzhou which ended without a solution. The Tibetans went back to enlisting more support for their cause, even to distant Beijing. With official help forthcoming, the Tibetans, led by the Nulra tribe, attacked and routed the Hui at first, but were nearly annihilated in retaliation. The Qinghai army's occupation was made secure, for the moment. Jamyang Shaypa went into exile to Nulra in the grasslands south of Hezuo, and, the missionaries report, enjoyed at least nominal protection of the Chone forces. The Tibetans continued to plan to retake Labrang, and went on to assemble an army. The Christian missionary and Tibetologist Robert Ekvall wrote:

> The following story describes the tense atmosphere. The Griebenows crossed the Minshan Range and, in a month-long journey, moving with haste and rarely taking even a single day's layover, had traced a great arc through hitherto unknown country. Their reports named ethnic groups, villages, encampments, and monasteries; told

One unit of the Labrang Tibetan militia, 1932.

of hostility and unexpected friendliness, of arrogance and suspicion on the part of chiefs and high lamas; and everywhere rumors of robbers—but no sightings. The weather had been pitiless—drenching rain in the valleys, driving hail in the higher grasslands, heat and thirst in one expanse of the desert.[165]

Apa Alo, acting as military commander, eventually demanded the withdrawal of all the Xining Hui troops from Labrang and the reduction of Ma Qi's exorbitant taxes. In response the Hui troops terrorized the Tibetan countryside. In July 1925, for example, they burned some sixty-seven villages and grasslands. For the Tibetans in and around Labrang, 1925 and 1926 were terrible years. Meanwhile, Apa Alo sought help wherever he could find it. During this period Labrang's marketplaces were stilled; it is likely that the prospect of loss of lucrative trade opportunities gave all sides at least pause prior to their invasions of Labrang.

The Mas attempted to conquer the Tibetans in 1925-1927, but the Tibetan militias had retreated to their familiar environment, the high mountains, and evaded their Hui adversaries. However, the promised Chinese help to the Tibetans never materialized, and the Hui troops retook Labrang, and this time, in 1926, they

> set up machine guns and mowed down as many of the fleeing monks as they could. On the heels of their victory, the Muslims set about exterminating the Tibetans with a ready will... [with numerous atrocities]. The Tibetans and the Muslims were engaged in ethnic slaughter, not modern warfare. Ma is said to have offered a reward for every Tibetan head his soldiers could bring in, while the Tibetans swooped down on any small concentrations of Hui to perform murders of great barbarity.... The Tibetans had clear superiority over the Muslims in numbers, but they lacked even the rudiments of strategy. In addition, their

loosely organized, lineage-based military structure made coordinated campaigning impossible. Their weapons were generally primitive, musket loaders and swords against the Hui machine guns.[166]

The next years saw warfare among the Hui, skirmishes with the Tibetans,[167] and periodic clashes between Muslim forces and the "Christian General" Feng Yuxiang's Chinese Nationalist Army (Guominjun) led by Liu Yufen.[168] Gansu in 1926 was racked by continuous warfare and terrorism perpetrated by Hui, Tibetans, and Feng's Chinese Nationalist Army, by smaller groups of bandits, and by individuals.

As if conditions were not bad enough, a major earthquake hit Gansu in May of 1927; it was particularly destructive in Chinese and Hui territories. The Chinese were starving, often conscripted by the army or by bandits, and were victims of systematic crimes perpetrated by roving gangs of murderers and thieves.[169] The battles of this time were often indecisive, though extremely bloody on all sides.

All of the political wrangling and battles among the Hui tribal groups, Chinese, and Tibetans naturally affected the Griebenows, albeit indirectly.[170] During the years of the worst Hui hostilities (1918-1927), the Hui forces did cause a measure of insecurity, but as the Griebenows gradually established their good reputation among the local peoples, they managed to retain a sense of security. However, the political and military environment became so unstable in 1927 that all missionaries were ordered to evacuate.

Blanche Griebenow and others mention battles between the Muslims and Tibetans; they cite an "anti-foreign feeling," but note that Labrang was "largely unaffected by conditions in central China."[171] On June 9, 1927, the Griebenows fled Labrang for a furlough in the USA and were allowed to return in October 1928 to what was considered a "safe" environment. Yet Robert Ekvall wrote to the contrary in his letter to Robert Carlson:

For a time the consular authorities flatly refused to allow us to leave the comparative safety of the river port Hankow, and only after much argument did they modify that prohibition into a grudgingly conceded at-your-own-risk permission; but precious days had been wasted.

Throughout that long day, we picked up vague rumors about a Muslim rebellion which had broken out in Kansu earlier in the year; but officially were assured that it had been suppressed easily, and the rebel leader, with a few remaining followers, had been driven into the western desert where they had most certainly perished.

Success in finding and engaging six large freight carts again put us on the go, riding on top of very carefully loaded-for-balance luggage. On the upgrade our slow advance became a halt as trace teams, working in relays, moved the carts in a stop-and-go routine.

So we moved across a desolate landscape into: a developing winter; a steady gain in altitude; and a ceaseless Siberian wind—which had picked up and carried sand from the Gobi, scoured the open fields, or dipping into the cart track trench, raised talcum-fine "yellow earth" into swirling clouds within which humans and animals struggled to move and breathe, and finally followed us to the high passes to hurl snow and ice crystals in our faces—until it indeed seemed that time and elements were combined against us. Grim demographic desolation also haunted the land, for everywhere famine was a threat.[172]

The group continued its slow move towards Gansu, hearing more and more rumors of the Muslim rebellion. Finally, nearing Longxi, they encountered the Hui forces. They received safe-conduct passes through the army lines. They witnessed a battle between the Hui and the provincial Chinese troops, with sabre-wielding cavalry charging against machine guns. Finally, just before Christmas, they reached Longxi, the westernmost CMA mission station.

The two-mule carriage en route, Blanche and son on foot.

At that point the company divided, with the Griebenows heading for Labrang...

The turmoil in the Muslim and immediately surrounding areas continued for some months, with number-less villages burned, and untold thousands of people slaughtered. As far as I know, Labrang escaped relatively unscathed.[173]

In her memoirs, Blanche Griebenow tells the story of her

family's return to Labrang after their first furlough in 1927. They were spared by the Muslim forces, but often found themselves battered between the Muslim and Chinese armies.

> We had quite a trip to Labrang. We never knew when we would see part of that [Muslim] army again. When we got to Labrang, we found out that they [the Muslims] had been there. Fearful that the Nationalist [Chinese] army would go to the mountains surrounding our house and fire down and kill their valuable horses, they [the Muslims] had tied the horses inside our living room and dining room. They were there for two days and one night. They emptied the books from our bookcases and used the bookcases for feeding troughs for the horses. Our books were ready for a bonfire when we got home. Everything was lost. The local people realized that our house had been occupied—the gates and doors were not locked when the army left—so they came in and looted to their full desire. Imagine our house when we returned from furlough![174]

During the years of the Qinghai army's siege of Labrang,

> the economic situation was getting more and more chaotic. The only solid currency was silver and the value of paper money fluctuated in relation to the fluctuations in value of silver dollars. The differences in exchange rates between Kansu and Szechuan were such that it was profitable for traders to buy silver in Kansu, travel to Sungp'an in northern Szechuan, sell the silver for paper, then return to Kansu to buy more silver. Or perhaps they would deal in opium also.[175]

With this situation in which large amounts of silver were being carried through the grasslands, particularly the uninhabited areas, robberies became more and more common. Contrary to the way such crimes had previously been carried out, thieves took to setting up an ambush along the trail and shooting travellers without warning from their concealed positions.[176]

Meanwhile, Apa Alo's response to the chaos in the region was to join an alliance of Feng's Nationalist Army under the command of Liu Yufen, local Lanzhou militiamen, and more ethnic Tibetan militiamen who were ready to fight again.[177] The Fifth Jamyang Shaypa and his family, escorted by the Tibetan Nulra, the Ninth Panchen Lama from Xining, Feng's Nationalist Army troops, and the Mongols all confronted the Hui forces.[178] In early 1927, Ma Qi, seeing that he could not defeat the unified opposition, capitulated, relinquished control of Labrang, and returned to Xining. The Tibetans got what they wanted—autonomy from Ma Qi. Finally, after more than eight years of bloodshed, Jamyang Shaypa returned to Labrang as religious and secular leader.[179] He had fled Labrang in the spring of 1925 and returned in triumph in June of 1927,[180] at which time the Tibetans felt certain of their autonomy.[181] Further, the Alos attempted to establish a defense alliance among many of Labrang's local clans.[182] Tibetan control over Labrang in 1927 seemed to solve Labrang's problems with the Hui, at least temporarily, and hopefully for the foreseeable future.[183]

In spite of the apparent calm, the Alos' optimism was tested in late 1927 and January 1928, when another Hui force once again went on the rampage against Labrang. They were brutal in their attack and looted and burned parts of Labrang before they moved west.

Warfare between the Qinghai and Gansu Muslims and their Muslim, Tibetan and Chinese adversaries was as widespread as ever,[184] and in April 1928 the Qinghai Muslims threatened Labrang.[185] The Labrang Tibetans, led by Apa Alo and Gonpo Dondrup, decided to seek Chinese aid in addition to alliances with Tibetan militias,[186] a decision not acceptable to all Tibetans.[187] Still, of all the possible choices, a defense treaty with the Nationalist Chinese government to complement the strength of the Tibetan militias was the best option. The alliance resulted in a supervised garrison of Chinese troops and an officially recognized Chinese title in the Gansu Provincial Army for Apa Alo, guarantees of heightened security for Labrang against the many marauding armies in the region. Apa Alo was appointed Labrang Security Officer by the Chinese in 1928,[188] and in 1934 he was promoted to Gansu Province Security Officer. This proved successful, and prevented hostile forces from destroying Labrang.[189] Another part of the agreement was that the Qinghai-Gansu border would be shifted so that in the eyes of the Nationalist Chinese Labrang Monastery would be in Gansu, not in Qinghai as before. When the Xining and Xunhua regions were detached from Gansu in 1928 and added to Qinghai, the Ma family immediately acquired dominance in Qinghai. This shift strengthened Apa Alo's position, and enabled him to get more aid from Lanzhou at the same time as weakening the Ma family's influence in Gansu.

In addition to the 1928 change in the Qinghai-Gansu boundary, the Chinese attempted to reduce the discord in Amdo in 1931 by designating fourteen tribal groups as "Fan," or Tibetan. This amounted to official recognition of the Labrang Tibetans by the Nationalists, though it was an attempt to categorize the Tibetans in Chinese terms.[190] The Gansu provincial government, now owing allegiance to Chiang Kai-shek and the Nationalist Party, included Labrang in the Chone district. However, it was classified only as an "appended district" of Chone, and under the leadership of Apa Alo, the only non-Chinese member of the provincial committee.

The new designation and the effectiveness of the alliance with the Chinese were tested in 1930-1931 when another branch of the Ma family attempted to occupy Labrang. This takeover attempt was quickly eliminated by the arrival of a number of Chinese armies from the east after the defeat of Feng Yuxiang by Chiang Kai-shek in the "Central Plains"

war in 1930. The allied forces of Tibetans and Chinese at Labrang in the late 1920s and early 1930s proved to be successful, creating the relatively calm atmosphere the Griebenows described. The Tibetans regained Labrang, but the price was that they had to work with the Chinese. Gonpo Dondrup and Apa Alo, no strangers to the Chinese, sought and welcomed their presence.

Apa Alo wrote that in 1928 the entire family went back to Labrang. They discovered that more Muslims had settled in Labrang town and were providing goods and services, promoting economic growth at Labrang and economic exchanges between Linxia, Labrang, and Xunhua. These newly arrived Muslim settlers remained undisturbed by the returning Tibetans.[191] Again, the Tibetans and Muslim Hui had developed a thriving wool business at Labrang that carried on during and after 1927-1928 in spite of or in the midst of chaos. The fact that Labrang had become an economic base for the Hui was doubtless an incentive to spare it from the devastation that hit other regional centers in the 1930s and 1940s.

During the rise and decline of Hui power at Labrang the monastery continued to function as a Tibetan Buddhist religious center. Even though there was fierce fighting going on very close by during these years,[192] life at Labrang carried on relatively undisturbed, as noted by the Griebenows. There was turbulence at Labrang, but from 1928 on the fundamental religious and secular integrity of the monastery, its properties, and lay settlements were not destroyed or dissipated until after 1949.

The end of the fighting did not immediately mean the end of hardship. The years 1926 to 1930 were famine years in Gansu, because of intense warfare in the region, lack of rainfall, sale of grain to China, and the promotion of opium production instead of grain production.[193] Many sources mention the high quality and widespread use of opium products in Gansu by the Chinese and some Hui. The natural disasters, the opium trade, and the attraction of Gansu's natural resources (coal, oil, and minerals) only made the situation worse—poor harvests, hunger, earthquakes, and the drug trade gave bandits and regional armies incentives to commit acts of violence.[194]

The region outside of Labrang was as dangerous as ever; in March 1930 it was still unsafe to travel outside of the immediate vicinity of the town.[195] In response, Labrang formed good relationships with Chone, under Yang Jiqing, who commanded the Taomin security forces (i.e., from Taozhou and Minxian) beginning in 1930. Yang was a "local administrator" (*tusi*) in the Chinese system, who pledged support for Labrang. This fact, combined with the Alos' liaisons with the Lanzhou authorities and other clan affiliations, bolstered Labrang's military strength.[196]

In May 1930, two years after their defeat by the Tibetans, the Hui of Lintan (Taozhou Old City) rebelled against their Tibetan overlords. The Hui succeeded in driving the Tibetans from the town and destroyed a large number of Tibetan and Chinese settlements around Lintan. The Hui then controlled the town for a month until the Gansu Nationalist army attacked and burned Lintan city, killing everyone and everything possible. Refugees from the town were nearly annihilated by the very Tibetans they had recently routed.[197] Bandits soon took the opportunity presented by the battles to loot and burn nearby Taozhou New City.

Battles between Hui, Tibetans, and Chinese continued, and there were alliances between the Chinese and the Hui, but the core of Muslim Hui power was finally destroyed in the 1930s because of divisiveness between different Muslim groups and sustained civil war. Still, bandits roamed Amdo, and the Tibetans, Hui, and Chinese fought each other with ferocity throughout the 1930s and 1940s. With the exception of the Qinghai military occupation in 1925-1927, Labrang was largely spared the worst of the revolutions and terror that ravaged central China so extensively in the early twentieth century.[198]

In 1933 Apa Alo attended a major political meeting in Nanjing and explained Labrang's circumstances to Chiang Kai-shek, Wang Jingwei, Zhu Peide and other leaders of China's Nationalist regime. He described the weakening but persistent harassment by the Qinghai Hui army and its attempts to annex Labrang outright, regardless of the 1927 Chinese-negotiated border shift.[199] The meeting unfortunately had few positive results. Other important issues in the 1933 meeting and in the following years concerned Labrang Monastery's assertion of property ownership, taxation privileges and precedents.[200] These problems were often discussed in the new political contexts sought by Apa Alo, but warfare between local nomads and neighboring Hui continued to obstruct Tibetan unity.[201]

China's ongoing warfare intruded on Labrang again when the troops of Chiang Kai-shek and Ma Lin moved into the Labrang area to attack the Chinese Communists on the Long March, then passing through the Tibetan highlands. Apa Alo and Labrang were visited by a large army of Nationalist troops in pursuit of Mao Zedong and his Communist Red Army. In his 1989 account, Apa Alo wrote that when faced with the decision to choose between helping the Nationalists or the Communists, he chose the Communists. He wrote that he considered and weighed his father's old Qing ties, and his own Republican and Communist contacts, and though aware of the location of both armies, he boldly denied having seen Mao Zedong or knowing the whereabouts of the Red Army's troops. Instead, Alo sent a messenger on horseback to warn the Red Army in nearby Lintan (Taozhou Old City) not to travel northwest but due west to avoid the superior Nationalist army. The Communists followed his advice, thereby avoiding almost certain defeat.[202] A Nationalist attack on the exhausted Red Army at that moment, in the Gansu highlands, could have meant a decisive defeat for the Communists. Labrang's allegiance was with the Communist forces, a fact that was to serve them well in later years.[203]

Apa Alo further affirmed Labrang's support of the Communists at least nominally in 1935 by sending a small Tibetan delegation to the northern divisions of the Red Army on their Eastern Expedition against Japan and the warlords in north China.[204] His son led the Tibetans and was compelled to spend a harsh winter on the front in 1935-1936,

during which he contracted a fatal illness and died shortly thereafter. Though not of great significance in the war, these events proved to be of vital importance for the history of modern Labrang, for they record alliances and Tibetan lives lost in defense of the Chinese Red Army.

Even if Apa Alo may have in retrospect embellished his role as a Communist supporter, the fact is that he was an intelligent military and political leader in early twentieth-century Labrang who shifted alliances to meet changing circumstances. He negotiated with the Chinese warlords, the Nationalists, and later the Communists, but always on behalf of the Tibetans' and his family's interests. He likely considered his and Labrang's interests as identical.

The Fifth Jamyang Shaypa, ca. 1932.

VI.

CONTINUITY AND CHANGE:

RELIGIOUS AND SECULAR EDUCATION

During the early decades of the twentieth century a number of unprecedented advances in education were attempted and realized at Labrang and in its territories. By no means did all Tibetan Buddhist monasteries have effective infrastructures or curricula for public education, but the evidence confirms that Labrang was progressive with regard to religious and lay education.

Labrang Monastery, with its libraries, its famous lineages of teachers and their disciples and its practice of public debate, exemplified Tibetan monastic education at its best. Although not all monks were good scholars or self-motivated and self-disciplined individuals (as in any educational institution), Labrang maintained rigorous courses of study.

The monastery was in effect a university divided into colleges, with different specialties and courses of study in each one, based on the classical Indian Buddhist model. The special fields were in all Buddhist sciences, the study and practice of Buddhist *sūtra*s and *tantras*, and the entire range of associated meditations, medicine, arts and humanities. Most of these specialties were housed in their own buildings and facilities at Labrang. The curriculum included fully developed courses, debates, and ritual practices. All courses functioned on a strict lunar calendrical system, observing all major Buddhist festivals and commemorations through-

out the year in addition to special events that required religious recognition. The specific content of the curriculum was broad-based, including memorization of and debate on major Buddhist *sūtras*, the teachings of the Buddhist "Middle Way" (*madhyamaka*), epistemology (*pramāṇa*), monasticism and ethics (*vinaya*), categories of selves, persons, and things, and the levels of consciousness (*abhidharma*), the wisdom literature (*prajñāpāramitā*), the entire system of

Young monks in a routine assembly.

Buddhist *tantras*, astrology, medicine, and other topics.[205] There were regular classes, examinations, and degrees awarded in these subjects.[206]

Though it had roots in the orthodox Gelukpa tradition of central Tibet, Labrang Monastery was not a strictly sectarian institution. In addition to the prominent central Tibetan Gelukpa systems, Labrang housed specialists in the older Tibetan Nyingma systems and accommodated theories and techniques from all the Tibetan Buddhist lineages. The abbotship rotated every three years, a procedure designed to protect against the development of prejudiced interests in the monastic administration. Though pluralistic in its academic approach, monastic education was not available to everyone throughout the extended community.

Religious specialists doing their rituals. Their long hair is wound under their headcoverings. Given the statue of Padmasambhava, the mythical founder of the Nyingma order, and the ritual dagger in front of the shrine, these richly clothed Tibetans are likely from the Nyingma order of Tibetan Buddhism. Even though Labrang Monastery was a bastion of the orthodox Gelukpa order, the institution's diversity is attested here.

There were at least seven major religious festivals in the monastic calendar year during which the monastery and grounds were open to the public. Many thousands of Tibetans would come to Labrang for these festivals, camping on the banks of the river, prostrating themselves and praying in the hundreds of temples and shrines, viewing the ceremonial monastic dances, and participating in the secular ones. Travel or pilgrimage to sacred sites was an important part of Tibetan Buddhist religion. The repertoire of religious practices at Labrang included a variety of local and borrowed beliefs and practices. At Labrang Monastery there were shamans and healers, Tibetan non-Buddhist Bon practitioners, propitiation of non-Buddhist deities, and beliefs in a wide range of myths. At the core of this array stood a Tibetanized model of an Indian Buddhist monastery. Thus, though the most esoteric rituals were reserved for monastic experts, some of the highlights were shown to the public to indicate the presence of the divine in their midst. These public rituals were considered by lay people to bestow good luck; by seeing the deities, pilgrims were in turn seen by and thus blessed by them.

Development of the monastic schools did not cease in the twentieth century. In 1939, the Fifth Jamyang Shaypa established the Upper Tantric College (*Gyuto*) at Labrang, after the Lhasa model. The Fifth Jamyang Shaypa also attempted to modernize the curriculum at Labrang by including secular studies imported from China. His incorporation of new ideas was an attempt to upgrade Labrang's curricula and practices. Additionally, the Fifth Jamyang Shaypa is known for his efforts to preserve Tibet's literary heritage by his continuing search for, collection, and preservation of rare Tibetan Buddhist manuscripts in the large library at Labrang.[207] His achievements were substantial in terms of his enthusiastic support of both the monastic curricula and lay education.

A narrator at New Year's festivities.

A Tibetan prognosticator flanked by two associates, possibly students or family members. He wears the white robes of a lay religious practitioner and has his long hair braided and rolled on his head. As elsewhere in Tibet, Western hats were very much in style at Labrang.

Gonpo Dondrup, early 1940s. By the 1940s New Year celebrations at Labrang had evolved into grand festivals with guests from Tibet and China. The Chinese word in back of Gonpo Dondrup means "long life" (shou).

Tibetan women's headgear, made of semi-precious stones, silver and metals, and long braids. These heavy ornaments signified wealth and prestige.

Tibetan women with straw for livestock. The lives of these women were quite different from the relatively privileged lifestyles of wealthy Tibetan women and the more independent nomads.

Blanche Griebenow in a field of oil-producing rape-seed in bloom, ca. early 1940s.

Looking over the monastery wall from the outside.

A typical nomad family in front of their yak-wool tent, with bags of wool and a butchered sheep.

An assembly of Labrang's monastic and lay communities.

Apa Alo and his sister Asur (?), early 1940s.

Alak Gungtang Tshang (?).

A folk dancer, in the Tibetan operatic tradition.

A public ritual dance ('chams).
New construction outside of Labrang.

A local Tibetan friend of the Griebenows. This woman wears a decorated amulet box around her neck. Her dress and jewelry suggest that she is a member of the sedentary Labrang community.

This upper-class woman is dressed in the fur-lined brocades, metal ornaments, and semi-precious stones that identify her as a Tibetan noblewoman. She stands on a woven wool carpet in front of a decorated tent.

A group of visiting nomads preparing food outside of the monastery compound.

Gonpo Dondrup's wife Guru Lhatso (R) and her daughter Asur (L).

A Tibetan prognosticator, one of many in residence at Labrang Monastery. This man, and others like him, is an unordained religious professional with his long hair braided and wound on top of his head. This unidentified man appears in many of the Griebenow photographs, and from the terse captions was a friend of the family but not a Christian convert.

A young woman from the Labrang community with typical dress and hairstyle.

Visiting Tibetan nomads come to Labrang for trade and pilgrimage. This couple do not display the wealth of other Tibetans, and do not wear the yakskin garments of the nomads. They are probably local residents engaged in farming or estate service.

Two Tibetans, perhaps a mother and daughter, wear the clothing and ornaments of sedentary and relatively wealthy Tibetans.

A wooden pole bridge near Labrang.

Tibetans at Labrang. Their clothing identifies them as local, and likely sedentary farmers or business people. The men wear Western-style brimmed hats and the women high-brimmed fur hats. At least some of these people are literate.

A Tibetan nomad, another unidentified but frequent visitor to the Griebenow home. He wears typical dress, with a fur pelt as decoration.

Tibetan guests from the Labrang community. Their dress identifies them as sedentary Tibetans.

The highlands south of Labrang
Monastery.

Marion Griebenow with monks from
Labrang.

A partial view of the CMA mission.

A Labrang monk, a nomad, and a local Tibetan at the CMA mission.

An unidentified Tibetan woman and child with Western-style hats visiting the Griebenows.

Tibetan nomads outside of Labrang.

A view of the CMA mission in the foreground, with Labrang Monastery in the distance.

A Muslim noodle-seller with a portable noodle bar in Labrang's marketplace. Tibetan women look on from the background.

A 'chams dance in the courtyard of the Main Assembly Hall.

The community gathers for a ritual performance in the courtyard of the Main Assembly Hall.

Monks debating in the Summer Garden, Labrang. The trees within Labrang's walls surround this open shrine and courtyard. Monks gather here as part of their curriculum to debate their lessons.

The monastery's resources were not reserved for the monastic community. There were rituals that the public participated in, and periodic public teachings. The general public likely did not understand the full significance of the elaborate rituals, and the teachings were most often beyond the comprehension of the average Tibetan.

In the 1930s and 1940s Labrang not only maintained monastic education, but also pursued initiatives in public

Monks performing tantric visualization rituals, here clad in "deity clothing" (lha chas), strange hats and ornate vestments. These ordained monks practice in front of a Buddhist stupa, a symbol of Buddhist attainment of enlightenment.

schooling. After the 1927 war period, monastery officials made attempts to introduce a new secular school system at Labrang and in its territories in which the participants would study Tibetan and Chinese languages, cultures, and histories.[208] There was in this context a self-conscious effort to promote the instruction of Tibetan language and culture in the local schools. Though the success of these efforts was intermittent they demonstrate that the monastic and secular elite had aspirations for development.[209]

There is some concrete evidence of these efforts in Apa Alo's memoirs. He wrote that one of the academic innovators and an ally of the Tibetans was Xuan Xiafu. This Chinese friend was active in promoting education in Labrang and Amdo, and was especially loyal to the Alos. He was an early Nationalist Party member who later became a member of the Chinese Communist Party; in the late 1920s he also worked for Feng Yuxiang.[210] In the late 1920s Xuan Xiafu used his influence to get Apa Alo membership first in Nationalist Party's Youth Corps, and then in the Lanzhou branch of the Party Committee.

On a different front, the Nationalist Youth Corps was supported by the Labrang Tibetans. The Youth Corps branch at Labrang promoted education, including Tibetan folk music and dance.[211] The branch published a bulletin[212] in which Apa Alo once introduced a proposal for a Tibetan nomad grasslands region crossing the boundaries of the Chinese provinces into which it had been divided—Gansu, Qing-hai, and Sichuan. He argued that the Tibetan grasslands already represented a real political unit and deserved official recognition.[213] Though ambitious, these efforts were also short-lived.

In 1928 two new schools were established in Golok territories, and the area's first girls' school was opened in 1940. There were only about twenty students at first, and never a large number, but enrollment gradually increased with several Tibetan, Chinese and Hui students.

New Year celebration. Marion Griebenow wrote: "Labrang, Tibet, 9 March 1923. We have just had a big (New Year's) fair at the temple a few days ago. Thousands of people were present at some of the sights. One forenoon, they had a large canvas picture of Buddha on display, and there were estimated to be twenty thousand or more to witness and worship it. The picture was let down on the side of a hill, and people were standing all around. Another day they had a dance which was quite a sight. The dancers were dressed in costumes which represent figures of worship. On the third day, in the evening, about a hundred figures made of butter, barley flour, and paints were on display all around a large building. These figures showed much care and skill in the making. It snowed that evening, and this glittering effect set them off beautifully in the light of the torches."

These accounts of the Tibetan educational initiatives sound nearly too good to be true, and there is no doubt that they were historically recent, prototype-style programs. The interesting point is, however, that they did happen, they were innovative, and they reveal a genuine interest in educational development on the part of the ruling elite at Labrang.

Dancers, sometimes part of the audience of a religious ritual. These dancers performed in the streets informally and at times as part of the lay audience.

A Tibetan ritual role, a "scapegoat" (glud rdzong) is a part of a ritual involving a designated person who signifies the community ridding itself of the past year's bad luck. From first-hand accounts written by M.G. and Blanche Griebenow in 1934 and 1939 : "In a dream, the Dalai Lama saw a demon about to do him great harm and bring great calamity to Tibet. The next morning he related the story to his advisors and the magicians and sorcerers announced that a man must be chosen to represent the demon, who must be dressed to resemble the evil spirit of the dream. Great gifts were to be given. To determine whether the gifts were sufficient, dice were to be cast. If the dice fell in favor of the Dalai Lama, the 'demon man' was to flee with what had been given him. If otherwise, more gifts were to be given until the dice should be favorable to the Dalai Lama. The 'demon-man' makes one think of the two-faced, crooked old devil himself in his costume, which is all white on the right side, and all black on the left. Even the skin on his face and hands is painted white and black."
Blanche Griebenow adds: "A Tibetan man is chosen each year to play the part of the devil. One-half of his body from head to foot is covered with white garments, while the other half is dressed in black. Even his face is painted white and black to correspond. He receives little gifts of coins and grain as an offering for taking away the sins of the Tibetan people in Labrang for each past year. Crowds follow him yelling and running, throwing stones at him as he nears the edge of the monastery precincts, in order to get him away quickly."

The Ceremony Courtyard (ston chos ra). Located next to the Maitreya Temple, this open shrine and courtyard was used as a site for different rituals. These were often elaborate, sometimes with powerful musical accompaniment, colorful, deeply symbolic, and usually with very striking costumed celebrants. Here is a monastic ritual dance being performed by young monks (phrug gar).

VII.
CHALLENGE AND SURVIVAL:
LABRANG IN RETROSPECT

The Griebenows' photographic and written "windows" into Labrang Monastery and its territories provide glimpses of a people and culture located at the crossroads or on the boundaries of four classical Asian civilizations. Though Tibetan, Labrang had an organic connection to the Mongols and extensive trade relations, military alliances, and conflicts with both the Hui Muslims and the Chinese.

If Labrang was an autonomous region, what were the roles of the Muslim Hui, the Chinese, and the Mongols? Concise answers to these questions require detailed analysis of each place through history; this book has only indicated some of the complexity present in pre-Communist Labrang. Muslim Hui cultures were a powerful and ethnically distinct force in the Labrang region. China was a primary trading partner and maintained relations with the Labrang Tibetans in many capacities. There were Chinese merchants in business at Labrang, Chinese craftsmen, Chinese soldiers, and diplomats. In the twentieth century the Mongol rulers in residence at Labrang were devout Tibetan Buddhists and at the same time political allies and subjects of the Tibetans. Labrang was a meeting point for these four and other groups. How did the Hui, Chinese, and Mongol peoples live with the Tibetans and maintain their ethnic identities and political structures? Did they manage to maintain their structures at all?

Monks announce the entrance of a religious person or the beginning of a ceremony with Tibetan shawms (rgya gling).

A brief answer is that the culture at Labrang was Tibetan, but its Tibetan ethnic identity underwent a superficial metamorphosis in order to communicate with the people beyond its very close borders,[214] much as the Chinese and Hui culture underwent changes on a special "middle ground." They did this in order to maintain trade, diplomatic, and military security. The Tibetans negotiated with the Chinese

The Fifth Jamyang Shaypa in ceremonial bone garments.

and entertained the Chinese diplomats and military officials as loyal allies and honored guests.

There was considerable interaction between Hui and Chinese. Hui, Chinese, and Tibetans intermarried, and diverse inheritance and religious guidelines for the children were established. As Griebenow wrote, "There are out there aboriginal tribes along the border who were Tibetan or Mongol Buddhists and are now Muslims, and some who were Muslim and are now Tibetan Buddhist."[215] This situation obviously made things more complex, since the Chinese had to deal with the Muslims as well as the Tibetans. Finally, the elite Mongols enjoyed some prestige at Labrang, since they were in fact among the historical founders of the community. The Mongol community was, however, mostly assimilated by the Tibetans, and in this respect quite different from the Hui and Chinese. Since the Mongols accepted the religious authority of the Tibetan Buddhist hierarchy at Labrang Monastery and supported the monastery financially, they were in turn more readily accepted by the Tibetans.

Labrang had the special kind of border culture that interfaced with its neighbors. There is no doubt that the agrarian Chinese lifestyles were in sharp contrast to Tibetan and Mongol nomad cultures, but there were also times when some Chinese engaged in sheep-herding and some Tibetans in agriculture and small business. The Tibetan borderland at Labrang contained a confluence of cultures in which the Chinese, Mongolian and Hui peoples conformed to the predominantly Tibetan ways. This statement, however, oversimplifies complex patterns of ethnic identities, political allegiances, and religious affiliations. For example, Chinese and Hui merchants and politicians visiting Labrang would act in ways they perceived to be Tibetan, but these attempts at assimilation were often based on

A public 'chams *dance.*

misapprehensions of Tibetan culture, which had the undesired effect of evoking misunderstanding and suspicion from the Tibetans, finally exacerbating relations. Further, permanent and semi-permanent Chinese and Hui residents of Labrang would adopt Tibetan culture superficially, but retain their own beliefs and practices in their own circles, which again had the effect of building invisible but very real barriers between cultures.

An Amdo Tibetan nomad woman in typical dress and hairstyle.

In conclusion, the story of the Alos both typifies and emphasizes Labrang's evolution as a part of the Tibetan nation at a confluence of tribal groups and political empires.[216] It is confirmed as such in the photographs, writings, and life stories of Blanche and Marion Griebenow. Labrang Monastery is located in what was then the remote hinterlands of Tibet, land controlled by fierce Tibetan nomads, though surrounded by the Hui to the northwest, Chinese to the east, and Mongols to the northeast. The monastic leaders managed to maintain Labrang's autonomy, however, until the invasions of the Red Army and subsequent destructive blows to Labrang Monastery, its institutions, libraries, and occupants. A fraction stands today, alive and growing, but it lives and grows in ways very different from the cultural and religious center that Marion and Blanche Griebenow came upon in the early 1920s.

It is undeniable that Labrang Monastery, its religious, artistic, and intellectual heritage were remarkable cultural achievements. Its border culture managed to survive in a multicultural environment while preserving its Tibetan identity by a combination of assertiveness and negotiations with its neighbors. Since its beginnings and especially in the modern period, its strongest allies were its Chinese neighbors, with whom the Labrang Tibetans managed to coexist. The monastery and community have changed significantly since the Chinese Communist period, but they survive. One can only hope that all of the peoples on this ethnic borderland will learn the lessons of mutual respect and appreciation, and let the monastery and its community assert itself in a manner consistent with its proud heritage.

Three familiar faces around the Griebenow household, ca. 1930.

A public dance in the courtyard of the Main Assembly Hall.

Notes and References

1. Some of the Griebenow photographs appear in Alak Shabdrung Tshang, *Thub bstan yongs su rdzogs pa'i mnga' bdag kun gzigs ye shes kyi nyi ma chen po 'jam dbyangs bzhad pa'i rdo rje 'pheng lnga'i rnam par thar ba mdor bsdus su bkod pa* [The Fifth Jamyang Shaypa, 1916-1947] (Nanjing, 1948). Some of the photos in the Griebenow Archve were not taken by the Griebenows. A few are attributed to other photographers, to Harrison Forman, for example, and others are anonymous.

2. The terms "ethnic groups," "tribal groups," "ethnic minorities," "clans" and "tribes" are all vague, technically incorrect, anachronistic terms. As a compromise I use "ethnic group," "tribe" and "tribal group" interchangeably. "Tribe" here refers to traditional units of peoples with common ancestry and with a respected internal autonomy. Its use does not imply that they were barbaric or that their political system was of lesser value than any other.

3. For concise definitions and histories of the Hui, Salars, Dongxiang and others see Jonathan Lipman, "The Border World of Gansu, 1895-1935" (Ph.D. diss., Stanford University; Ann Arbor: University Microfilms, 1981) and Dru Gladney, "Qingzhen: A Study of Ethnoreligious Identity among Hui Muslim Communities in China" (Ph.D. dissertation, University of Washington, Seattle; Ann Arbor: University Microfilms, 1987).

4. See especially Gladney, "Qingzhen," 6-63, 63 n. 1 and Lipman, "The Border World of Gansu," 36 n. 2, 45-64.

5. Compare the modern Western vision of Tibet, overstated as "a wondrous, unique civilization based wholly on the practice of Buddhism's highest ideals." Richard Gere, "Messages," in *Wisdom and Compassion: The Sacred Art of Tibet*, eds. Marylin Rhie and Robert Thurman (New York: Abrams, 1991), 8.

6. Huang Zhengqing, *Huang Zhengqing Yu Wushi Jiamuyang* (Lanzhou: Gansu People's Publishing Co., 1989), 7.12; cf. Huang Zhengqing, *Hvang krin ching blo bzang tshe dbang dang kun mkhyen lnga ba chen po sku mched zung gi rnam thar ba rjes su dran pa zag med ye shes kyi me long (A blo spun mched kyi rnam thar)*, trans. Klu tshangs rdo phrug (Beijing: People's Publishing House, 1994); Li An Che, *Labrang: A Study in the Field by Li An Che*, ed. Chie Nakane (Tokyo: Institute of Oriental Culture, The University of Tokyo, 1982). This book was outdated in 1982, but like other pioneering works contains some descriptions of Labrang in the 1930s. It has been reprinted as: Li An-che, *History of Tibetan Religion: A Study in the Field* (Beijing: New World Press, 1994). The first two books mentioned in this note are credited to Huang Zhengqing, Apa Alo, and are the Chinese and Tibetan versions of his memoirs. There are enough differences in the two versions to treat them as separate compositions.

7. Ray Hart, "Religious and Theological Studies in American Higher Education: A Pilot Study," *Journal of the American Academy of Religion* 59, quoted in Malcolm David Eckel, "The Ghost at the Table: On the Study of Buddhism and the Study of Religion," *Journal of the American Academy of Religion* 62/4 (Winter 1994): 1086.

8. Hart quoted in Eckel, 1086.

9. Hart quoted in Eckel, 1089.

10. See Franz Michael, *Rule by Incarnation: Tibetan Buddhism and Its Role in Society and State* (Boulder: Westview Press, 1982); and others.

11. Joseph Fletcher, "Ch'ing Inner Asia c. 1800," in *The Cambridge History of China*, Volume 10, Late Ch'ing, 1800-1911, Part I, eds. Denis Twitchett and John K. Fairbank (London: Cambridge University Press, 1978), 92-94. Labrang's ties to the central Tibetan authorities

are described in Huang, *rNam thar*, 92-96, Appendix. Note that this phenomenon of combined "religious and secular leaders" was also practiced in nearby Qinghai by the Muslims; see Lipman, "Ethnicity and Politics in Republican China: The Ma Family Warlords of Gansu," *Modern China* 10/3 (July 1984), 290 n. 4.

12. Fletcher, 92; Jo-Ann Gross, "Introduction," in *Muslims in Central Asia: Expressions of Identity and Change,* ed. Jo-Ann Gross (Durham and London: Duke University Press, 1992), 12, 14.

13. Huang, *rNam thar*, 248-249.

14. Fletcher, 101; D. Seyfort Ruegg, "*mchod yon, yon mchod* and *mchod gnas/yon gnas*: On the Historiography and Semantics of a Tibetan Religio-Social and Religio-Political Concept," in Ernst Steinkellner, ed., *Tibetan History and Language: Studies Dedicated to Uray Geza on His Seventieth Birthday* (Wien, Austria: Arbeitskreis für Tibetische und Buddhistische Studien, 1991), 441-454; note especially the considerations and bibliography on pp. 448-449 n. 29. The "lama-patron" (*yon mchod*) relationship was a crucial part of Tibetan politics and should not be underestimated. I only mention it briefly here; see the brief summary in Wolfgang von Erffa, *Uncompromising Tibet: Tradition-Religion-Politics* (New Delhi: Paljor Publications, 1996), 9-15; and others.

15. Huang, *Huang*, 69.

16. *Ibid.*, 6.14; the list is repeated in Huang, *rNam thar* and in Luo.

17. See Susan Naquin and Chun-fang Yu, eds., *Pilgrims and Sacred Sites in China* (Berkeley: University of California Press, 1992), 11: "...Chinese were by preference lowlanders...."

18. See Huang, *Huang*, 1-3; Huang, *rNam thar*; Li.

19. The eight auspicious symbols: *bKra shis rtags brgyad*: conch, umbrella, victory banner, fish, vase, wheel, knot of infinity, and lotus.

20. Brag dgon zhabs drung dkon mchog bstan pa rab rgyas, *Yul mdo smad kyi ljongs su thub bstan rin po che ji ltar dar ba'i tshul gsal bar brjod pa: Deb ther rgya mtsho* [The Ocean Annals of Amdo], reproduced by Lokesh Chandra, Śatapiṭaka Series, 226 (New Delhi, 1977), 2a3-4. (Hereafter referred to as *Deb ther rgya mtsho*.) rGyal srid rin chen sna bdun, the seven jewels of a king: *cakra*, the wheel [of law]; *hastin*, elephant; *aśva*, horse; *maṇi*, jewels; *mantrin*, minister; *senāpati*, general; *strī*, queen.

21. "In the northern part of a northern country the study and practice of the *Prajñāpāramitā* will flourish." *Deb ther rgya mtsho*, 2a3-4. According to the *lHa mo dri ma med pa'i 'od lung bstan pa*, "the *dharma* will flourish in the land of the red-faced ones 2500 years after the enlightenment." *Ibid.*, 2a3-4.

22. H.V. Guenther, "Buddhism in Tibet," in *Buddhism and Asian History*, eds. J.M. Kitagawa and M.D. Cummings (New York: Macmillan, 1989). In addition to the established religious traditions in Amdo, Labrang Monastery traces its roots to the re-establishment of Buddhism as a major institution in central Tibet by the Indian Atiśa Dipaṃkaraśrijñāna (982-1054), who contributed to the beginnings of the Kadampa order. It was this system that became the basis for the later Gelukpa order, and subsequently the core Buddhist curriculum at Labrang. The opening verses in the *Deb ther rgya mtsho*, perhaps the most famous history of Amdo, cite this prophecy: *bka' gdams bstan pa'i chu rgyun phyogs mthar rgyas pa'i rten 'brel du* ("There is a connection to the flow of Kadampa teachings, which spread throughout [the nation].") The Tibetan tradition records that the construction of Labrang was predicted both in the writings of Atiśa and in those of his disciple Dromdon; according to the predictions, Labrang Monastery would be built in the same manner and with the same affiliations as Reting Monastery in central Tibet (*Deb ther rgya mtsho*, 6b3). This prediction indeed came to pass with Labrang recognizing the authority of the Dalai Lamas and their disciples in central Tibet, and with the construction of buildings at Labrang modelled after those at Reting, Drepung, and other monasteries in central Tibet.

23. *Deb ther rgya mtsho*, 3a1.

24. *Ibid.*, 2b2-3a1.

25. Yon tan rgya mtsho [Yontan Gyatso], *Chos sde chen po bla brang bkra shis 'khyil: mkhas grub 'bum sde'i rol mtsho mdo sngags bstan pa'i 'byung gnas dga' ldan bshad sgrub bkra shis 'khyil gyi skor bzhad gzhung dal 'bab mdzod yangs las nye bar sgrub pa sngon med legs bshad ngo mtshar bkra shis chos dung bzhad pa'i sgra dbyangs* (Paris: n.p., 1987), 15.

26. The Dalai Lamas, the Jamyang Shaypas, and the large number of other "lineages of reborn Tibetan Buddhist lamas" are the institutionalization of the Buddhist belief that a spiritually advanced person can choose his or her birth in a succeeding lifetime. Hence, the Dalai Lama in the early twentieth century was the Thirteenth and

the Jamyang Shaypa the Fifth incarnations in those particular lines. The procedure for identifying reborn Buddhist lamas has been discussed elsewhere in detail. See John Avedon, *In Exile from the Land of Snows* (New York: Knopf, 1984); Franz Michael, *Rule by Incarnation: Tibetan Buddhism and Its Role in Society and State*; and others.

27. Mongolian sources identify this person as Boshugtu Jinong, but Erdeni may be a title added to Jinong, "Viceroy." Thanks to Christopher Atwood for information about the Mongols here and throughout, lexical suggestions, and clarification of key events in Chinese history.

28. 11th cycle, Earth Female Buffalo year, *Deb ther rgya mtsho*, 1a4-2a1; Yontan Gyatso, 29.

29. Huang, *Huang*, 5.14-6.1.

30. Here we have yet another claim of sovereignty in this region, in addition to the Chinese, Muslim, and Tibetan claims.

31. The "twenty-nine" refers to the twenty-nine separate "banners" or principalities among the Mongols of Qinghai. Kunga Paljor (Gungga Baljur), the prince of the Khoshud South Leading Banner (the official name of his principality) was the highest ranking, but he did not directly rule over the other twenty-eight princes.

32. Huang, *rNam thar*, 142.

33. Li, 27.

34. Compare the *menhuan* structure among Muslims in China. The ethnic minority identity and small-kingdom or semi-independent state situation functioned in similar ways in different cultures.

35. See Yontan Gyatso, 30.

36. See *ibid.*, 16.

37. Huang, *Huang*, 6.11; for detailed descriptions of the major structures in pre-Communist Labrang, see the *Deb ther rgya mtsho*; Tenzin Palbar, *Nga'i pha yul gyi ya nga ba'i lo rgyus* [The Tragedy of My Homeland] (Dharamsala: Narthang Publications, 1994); Heather Stoddard, *Le Mendiant de l'Amdo.* (Paris: Société d'Ethnographie, 1986); Yontan Gyatso; Alak Shabdrung Tshang; Li; Cao Ruigai, ed., *Labuleng Si* (Beijing: Cultural Publishing House, 1989); and others.

38. Huang, *Huang*, 2.

39. Huang, *rNam thar*, 239. Regents were appointed to handle monastery affairs during the period after the death of an incarnate lama and before the discovery of his successor.

40. After the death of the Fifth Jamyang Shaypa on April 14, 1947, the 9th Panchen Lama took over as regent once again, until the Sixth Jamyang Shaypa was enthroned.

41. Huang, *Huang*, 33.

42. *Ibid.*, 53.

43. Huang, *rNam thar*, 32-33.

44. "Study of Gansu's ethnic conflicts and compromises may enhance our understanding of peripheral China and peripheral Islam—a double-edged comprehension of perception and behavior on frontiers." Jonathan N. Lipman, "Ethnicity and Politics in Republican China," 289. I likewise suggest that study of Labrang will enhance our comprehension of the monastery itself and offer a quadruple-edged comprehension of perception of behavior on the frontiers.

45. The Ya gyal ldong family. See Yontan Gyatso; *Deb ther rgya mtsho*; Li, etc.

46. See Christopher I. Beckwith, *The Tibetan Empire in Central Asia: A History of the Struggle for Great Power among Tibetans, Turks, Arabs, and Chinese during the Early Middle Ages* (Princeton: Princeton University Press, 1987).

47. See Ruth W. Dunnell, *The Great State of White and High: Buddhism and State Formation in Eleventh-Century Xia* (Honolulu: University of Hawai'i Press, 1996).

48. See David D. Buck, "Introduction," *The Journal of Asian Studies* 53/1 (February 1994): 6; Benedict Anderson, *Imagined Communities* (London: Verso, 1995); see also Jo-Ann Gross, "Introduction," in *Muslims in Central Asia: Expressions of Identity and Change*, 5 n. 1; 6, 7, 12; A.P. Cohen, *The Symbolic Construction of Community* (Chichester: Ellis Horwood, Ltd.; London: Tavistock Publications, 1985), 12-13.

49. See Buck, 3-10.

50. See Huang, *Huang*, 61; Huang, *rNam thar*, 150.

51. *Deb ther rgya mtsho*, 4aff: Records from 650-839 CE, from the "Early Transmission" of Buddhism to Tibet from India, name this region of

Tibet mDo smad. The classical sources also give names to the different regions of mDo smad—Gyi thang (slightly north and northeast of Kokonor), gYer mo thang (west of Kokonor), and Tsong kha bde khams (further north and east of Kokonor). In contrast to this, some sources state that the entire mDo smad region is called Greater Tsong kha, and Lesser, or Northern Tsong kha. Still other sources state that the entire region is known as mDo khams, and is divided sometimes into six, or three regions, called respectively sMra khams for modern mDo khams, gYer mo thang for mDo smad, and Gyi thang for the Tsong kha region. Further, the Tsong kha region is itself sometimes divided into eighteen districts. All of these varying names have their stories, etymologies, and claims to sovereignty. The name "Amdo" has many etymologies, here the one that describes the region as extending from the Great "Ah" glacier on the east face of Bayanha Mountain (el. approx. 6,000 m.) which goes along the Sebo valley of the 'Bri chu, or Yangtze River, to the regions below ("mDo"), giving the name "Amdo." However, the area described by this etymology does not include all of the peoples and regions included in the broader historical Amdo.

52. See John D. Rogers, "Post-Orientalism and the Interpretation of Premodern and Modern Political Identities: The Case of Śrī Laṅkā," *The Journal of Asian Studies* 53/1 (February 1994): 15-16.

53. "The most important element of culture." Yihong Pan, "Sino-Tibetan Treaties in the Tang Dynasty," *T'oung Pao* 78 (1992): 122.

54. In addition to social and political classes there were numerous categories of religious practitioners called "Tibetan Buddhists." See, for example, Stanley Tambiah, *The Buddhist Saints of the Forest and the Cult of Amulets* (New York: Cambridge University Press, 1984); Reginald A. Ray, *Buddhist Saints in India: A Study in Buddhist Values and Orientations* (New York: Oxford University Press, 1994); and other books and articles on this topic.

55. It may well have been the case that other border cultures created further subgroups beyond the four here mentioned. This does not detract from the value of these categories included here, which are also cited in contemporary Chinese writings on Labrang. See Huang, *rNam thar*, 17-18, where the four are listed; Luo Faxi, ed., *Labuleng Si Gai Kuang* (Lanzhou: People's Publishing House, 1990); and other sources.

56. Huang, *Huang*, 6.25. Huang, *rNam thar*, 17: *sog po dang bod sku*

drag dang mi drag...

57. Like many of the other numbers cited, this quantity is a traditional number and technically inaccurate.

58. Huang, *Huang*, 7: "There were eleven Mongol 'arrows' and thirteen Tibetan villages in the vicinity of Labrang that were related to Labrang in this way." Listed on 7.2ff.

59. *Ibid.*, 7.5. Though cited in the sources, these distinctions are arbitrary. I do not include the Tibetan and Chinese terms in this brief account.

60. For information about the Salars, see Lipman, "The Border World of Gansu"; Dru Gladney; and others.

61. The "six hundred" is another arbitrary and inaccurate number. See Li; Jo-Ann Gross, ed., *Muslims in Central Asia: Expressions of Identity and Change* (Durham and London: Duke University Press, 1992), and others. See Pelbar, 19ff, for the Labrang region; see also the *Deb ther rgya mtsho*, and others for complete details.

62. Christian and Missionary Alliance maps #1, #2, and in numerous editions of the *Alliance Weekly*, etc.; glass lantern slide of regional map made by Marion Griebenow; Yontan Gyatso; and others. On the extent of Imperial Tibet, see Beckwith, *The Tibetan Empire in Central Asia*.

63. Li, 8.

64. "Further, in the greater Labrang region in the 1920s there were the eleven Mongol 'arrows,' the thirteen Tibetan villages, eighty affiliated ethnic groups, and some 800 merchant families." Huang, *rNam thar*, 34.

65. Lipman, "Ethnicity and Politics in Republican China," 286. Even though there were some sedentary Tibetans engaged in agriculture, trade, and religion, I simplify by associating the Tibetans with Lipman's "pastoral nomads" and the Chinese with "sedentary farmers."

66. Hajji Yusuf Chang, "The Hui (Muslim) Minority in China: An Historical Overview," *Journal of the Institute of Muslim Minority Affairs* 8/1 (January 1987): 68; see Mark Juergensmeyer, *Religious Nationalism Confronts the Secular State* (Delhi: Oxford University Press, 1994), 110-153 (originally published as *The New Cold War: Religious Nationalism Confronts the Secular State* [Berkeley: University of California Press,

1993]). The number of deaths is impossible to verify.

67. Huang, *Huang*, 37ff. The Chinese and Tibetan versions of this text contain detailed descriptions of these events. I include a brief account here, leaving a detailed analysis for another work in progress.

68. Lipman, "Ethnicity and Politics in Republican China," 290ff, 302.

69. *Ibid.*, 289.

70. *Ibid.*, 290ff.

71. Jonathan Lipman, "Ethnic Violence in Modern China: Hans and Hui in Gansu, 1781-1929," in *Violence in China: Essays in Culture and Counterculture*, ed. Jonathan N. Lipman and Steven Harrell (Albany: State University of New York Press, 1990).

72. 1870-1955; 55 years of missionary service; retired 1947.

73. William D. Carlsen, *Tibet: In Search of a Miracle* (New York: Nyack College, 1985), 36. Mentioned many times in Christian and Missionary Alliance publications and archives.

74. This story is told in many places in the CMA Archives and is well-known to former CMA missionaries.

75. Chone was an autonomous region led by ethnic Tibetan chieftains. The style of rulership at Chone was not entirely unlike the situation at Labrang, though authority structures were quite different.

76. Marion Grant Griebenow's personal file states that he "converted" on November 25, 1916 to evangelical Christianity from his parents' Presbyterian and later German Lutheran roots, and Blanche's states that she converted to the same from her family's Methodist affiliations in 1911. Unpublished Archive file, Christian and Missionary Alliance Headquarters, Colorado Springs, CO.

77. Carol Carlson, "Marion Grant Griebenow: His Goal," *The Alliance Witness*, December 6, 1972, 6-7; Blanche Willars Griebenow, *The Memoirs of Blanche Griebenow*, ed. Luke H. Sheng, unpublished, undated manuscript, compiled in Brighton, MI, ca. 1988, in the possession of Mei Griebenow, pp. 1-2. This passage is compiled from both sources.

78. Carol Carlson, 6-7; B.W. Griebenow, *The Memoirs of Blanche Griebenow*, 1-2. This passage is compiled from both sources.

79. Modern Wuhan includes three cities: Wuzhang, Hanyang, and Hanzhou.

80. B.W. Griebenow, *The Memoirs of Blanche Griebenow*, 9.

81. There are conflicting dates listed in CMA records. Several files and one of M.G. Griebenow's letters state that he and Blanche Willars reached their "fields" on January 2, 1922. Personal data files, CMA Archives, Colorado Springs, CO. Letter reproduced in B.W. Griebenow, *The Memoirs of Blanche Griebenow*, 21.

82. Taozhou New City, now simply "New City" a few miles away, was populated entirely by Chinese even then. This is an example of the proximity of Tibetan and Chinese cultures.

83. Published in 1949, but in rough draft, and revised by Griebenow in 1957.

84. M.G. Griebenow, March 1, 1922, unpublished letter reproduced in B.W. Griebenow, *The Memoirs of Blanche Griebenow*, 24-25.

85. *Ibid.*

86. *Ibid.*

87. *Ibid.*

88. *Ibid.*

89. *Ibid.*

90. *Ibid.* The missionary maps of this region always include Labrang and Amdo inside of Tibet. Also, see a similar map in David P. Ekvall, *Outposts or Tibetan Border Sketches* (New York: Alliance Press, 1906).

91. M.G. Griebenow, March 1, 1922, reproduced in B.W. Griebenow, *The Memoirs of Blanche Griebenow*, 24-25.

92. Blanche Griebenow, Reminiscences, March 1953, transcript of tape 2, side 1, p. 12. Taped in Nyack, NY, transcribed by Mei Griebenow, in the possession of Mei Griebenow.

93. M.G. Griebenow, unpublished letter, 1922, in CMA Archives, Colorado Springs, CO.

94. B. Griebenow, Reminiscences, March 1953.

95. *Ibid.*

96. *Ibid.*

97. *Ibid.*

98. George W. Griebenow, "Recollection of His Life in Tibet," taped December 27, 1983, Edina, MN, transcribed by Mei Griebenow, March 1989, in the possession of Mei Griebenow.

99. *Ibid.*

100. Robert and Connie Harrison, personal correspondence to Mei Griebenow, January 1992, in the possession of Mei Griebenow. Note that there was only minimal Russian contact with Labrang and as mentioned, the Mongols often assimilated Tibetan lifestyles, and were perhaps indistinguishable from ethnic Tibetans for the short-term visitor. Still, contact with Russians is mentioned and photographed in the Griebenow Archives. The locations the Harrisons use for the different ethnic groups are over-specific; there were Hui, Chinese, and Mongol groups in the region with no distinct separation of territories. Furthermore, the Harrisons fail to mention the active trade between the Tibetans and their neighbors and the intermarriage of Tibetans with Hui, Chinese and Mongols. Still, these accounts do show the Tibetan sense of their land and culture.

101. G. Griebenow.

102. *Ibid.* Here "equilibrium" means survival in their own places on their own terms.

103. The history of the Chinese Muslims is well-documented. See the interesting account of the region in Marion and Blanche Griebenow, et al., "A Foray Into Tibet: Young Alliance Missionaries in a New Pioneering Venture: Five Hundred Miles on Horseback Through the 'Forbidden Land,'" *The Alliance Weekly* (January 12, 1924): 743ff.

104. B.W. Griebenow, *The Memoirs of Blanche Griebenow*, 36.

105. *Ibid.*

106. Harrisons, personal correspondence to Mei Griebenow; Nita Fowler, conversation with Paul Nietupski, Colorado Springs, CO, January 1994. The blue color is cited in the early period in Blanche's reminiscences, and the blue appears in the color photographs taken in the mid-1940s. It therefore seems that blue paint or a blue "whitewash" was used when available.

107. G. Griebenow.

108. B. Griebenow, Reminiscences, March 1953.

109. *Ibid.*

110. Lois Kemerer, private correspondence to Mei Griebenow, December 8, 1991, 2.

111. Rev. Thomas Moseley, "Back to the Kansu-Tibetan Border," *The Alliance Weekly* (June 20, 1931): 401.

112. M.G. Griebenow, "Our Foreign Mail Bag," *The Alliance Weekly* (April 16, 1932): 250.

113. "The Gospel Trumpet Sounding in Labrang, Tibet," *The Alliance Weekly* (June 11, 1932): 376.

114. See Robert E. Ekvall, "The Opportunity in Northeast Tibet," *The Alliance Weekly* (August 27, 1927): 570ff. Marion Griebenow went on a long tour in November of 1933; see Ruth E. Lindstrom, "Missionary Mailbag," *Kansu-Tibetan Border News*, 1933, 2.

115. John O. Carlsen, "From the Kansu-Tibetan Border Mission," *The Alliance Weekly* (September 12, 1925): 626, 631.

116. Rev. Thomas Moseley, "A Night in a Tibetan Nomad Tent," *The Alliance Weekly* (December 2, 1933): 760.

117. M.G. Griebenow, "Our Tibetan Guests," *Kansu-Tibetan Border News* 1/5 (April 1935): 1-3.

118. *Ibid.*, 1-3.

119. Rev. William Christie, "Department of Prayer," *The Alliance Witness* (February 27, 1937): 137.

120. M.G. Griebenow, "Traveling with a God of Tibet," *The Alliance Weekly* (May 14, 1938): 312-314.

121. M.G. Griebenow, "Pioneering Up South," *The Alliance Weekly* (March 2, 1940): 136ff.

122. *Ibid.*

123. *Ibid.*

124. Blanche Willars Griebenow, et al., "West China Conference," *The Alliance Weekly* (January 13, 1940), 26.

125. M.G. Griebenow, "Journey to Sungpan," *The Regions Beyond: Newsletter of the Kansu-Tibetan Border Mission* 2/2 (1941): 10-13.

126. M.G. Griebenow, "Across China in Two Days," *The Alliance Weekly* (February 15, 1941): 104-105.

127. M.G. Griebenow, "A Living Buddha Dies," *The Alliance Weekly* (June 21, 1947): 393; also in the commemorative volume by Alak Shabdrung Tshang.

128. M.G. Griebenow, "Back in Labrang," *The Alliance Weekly* (October 18, 1947): 666.

129. M.G. Griebenow, "Taking Christ to Tibetan Nomads," *The Alliance Weekly* (February 1, 1947): 74-75.

130. Part of the spirit of the Griebenows is illustrated in the fact that from the beginning of their stay they had little regard for the risks of living and travelling in the region. M.G. Griebenow, "God's Miracle of Healing in Tibet," *The Alliance Weekly* (March 1950): 38, 44.

131. M.G. Griebenow, "Gospel Triumphs in Tibet," *The Alliance Weekly* (June 5, 1948): 361.

132. M.G. Griebenow, personal correspondence to Rev. A.C. Snead, March 14, 1949.

133. M.G. Griebenow, "Tibetan Prayer Conference," *The Alliance Weekly* (April 25, 1925): 282.

134. Here, as I mention above, I choose to use the Tibetan name "Alo" (*a blo*) for all members of this family for ease of reference, even though they had different personal names and titles. Though technically incorrect, I prefer this term to the Chinese "Huang" or their Tibetan clan name "dPal shul." See the story of their adoption of the Chinese surname "Huang," below.

135. Huang, *Huang*, 4.23. Here I only mention Zhao Erfeng briefly, even though his adventures into eastern Tibet were aggressive and brutal, and Gonpo Dondrup's accommodation of this individual ironic when seen in retrospect. Zhao's adventures signalled the beginning of Chinese movement into eastern Tibet.

136. Huang, *Huang* reads six children, but personal testimony mentions seven children.

137. Huang, *rNam thar*, 4. I follow the list of Gonpo Dondrup's (two) spouses and children as recorded by Apa Alo. However, Li states that Gonpo Dondrup had three wives.

138. Huang, *rNam thar*, 5.

139. Huang, *Huang*, 2. Asur's daughter is Namkho (Namgyal Wangmo).

140. See White's theory of "middle ground" between different peoples, created out of necessity, contorting their cultural lifestyles to accommodate the explosive potential border war problem. A "middle ground" is a ground of compromise that involves approximating the host cultures' customs. Visitors to Labrang's markets and temples doubtlessly changed their behavior to be acceptable to Labrang's religious institutions, and to the public to ensure productive deals with merchants. Richard White, *The Middle Ground: Indians, Empires, and the Republics in the Great Lakes Region, 1650-1815* (New York: Cambridge University Press, 1991), x, 2.

141. Huang, *Huang*, 3.15-16; Huang, *rNam thar*, 8.

142. There are similar photos in the Griebenow Archives.

143. The following description of ethnic sentiment closely matches that found among Labrang's Tibetans: "The 'commonality' which is found in community need not be a uniformity. It does not clone behavior or ideas. It is a commonality of forms (ways of behaving) whose content (meanings) may vary considerably among its members. The important thrust of this argument is that this relative similarity and difference is not a matter for 'objective' assessment: it is a matter of feeling, a matter which resides in the minds of the members themselves. Thus, although they recognize important differences among themselves, they also suppose themselves to be more like each other than like the members of other communities. But in even more naive manner, lay people 'understand' other people's kinship or familihood by assimilating it to their own. That is, they place their own interpretive constructions upon other people's experiences and frequently confuse the two. Of course, we have to use our own experience as the starting point in our attempts to make sense of what we see around us." Cohen, 20-21, 40.

144. Lipman "The Border World of Gansu," 88. Reference to Robert B. Ekvall, *Cultural Relations on the Kansu-Tibetan Border* (Chicago: University of Chicago Press, 1939).

145. See D.S. Ruegg, "Vajrayāna Buddhism in the Western Himālaya," *Acta Indologica* VI (1984): 370-371.

146. "Since Ming times the Hui spoke Chinese in addition to Arabic and Persian, wore Chinese dress, adopted Chinese names, married Chinese, and worked closely with the Han in military, political, agricultural and commercial fields. Physically, they became more similar to the Han than to other Muslim minorities." Chang, 69.

147. Lipman, "Ethnic Violence in Modern China: Hans and Hui in Gansu, 1781-1929," 83.

148. Described by the marriage of a Muslim groom to a Tibetan woman, each of whom maintained their respective religious affiliations. M.G. Griebenow, "Islam in Tibet," *The Moslem World* 26 (Hartford: Hartford Seminary Foundation, 1936), 127-129; see Lipman, "Ethnicity and Politics in Republican China," 288.

149. Lipman, "Ethnicity and Politics in Republican China," 306.

150. See Rev. Carter D. Holton, "The Salars of Kansu, West China," *The Alliance Weekly* (September 2, 1933): 552; Dr. Samuel M. Zwemer, "On the Frontiers of Northwest China," *The Alliance Weekly* (October 28, 1933): 680ff; entire issue, *The Alliance Weekly* (January 13, 1934). For a detailed account of the conflicts between the Muslims, the Chinese, and the Tibetans, with a focus on the Amdo Tibetans, see Palbar.

151. See Huang, *Huang*, 6-8.

152. James E. Sheridan, *China in Disintegration: The Republican Era in Chinese History, 1912-1949* (New York: The Free Press, 1975), 78-83. Missionary accounts from the area include numerous stories of barbarity and general lawlessness. For examples, see William Christie, "Christie Letters," unpublished manuscript, November 15, 1892, CMA Archives; numerous accounts in the *Alliance Weekly* and many other sources.

153. Lipman, "Ethnic Violence in Modern China," 72.

154. Sheridan, 59, 183ff.

155. *Ibid.*, 27-56; John K. Fairbank and Albert Feuerwerker, *The Cambridge History of China 13: Republican China 1912-1949, Part 2* (New York: Cambridge University Press, 1986), 27-125.

156. Sheridan, 58-59; see Gavan McCormack, *Chang Tso-lin in Northeast China, 1911-1928: China, Japan, and the Manchurian Idea* (Stanford: Stanford University Press, 1977).

157. W. Christie, "Christie Letters," unpublished manuscript, 1915, CMA Archives.

158. Huang, *Huang*, 7.

159. *Ibid.*, 8-9; Huang, *rNam thar*, 22-23.

160. Huang, *Huang*, 2.24-3.9.

161. A.J. Fesmire, "New Openings in Tibet," *The Alliance Weekly* (August 5, 1922).

162. M.G. Griebenow, "Tibetan-Border Blessings," *The Alliance Weekly* (August 5, 1922).

163. Huang, *rNam thar*, 40.

164. *Ibid.*

165. Robert Ekvall quoted in Robert Carlson, private correspondence to CMA Headquarters, undated, CMA Archives.

166. Quoted from Jonathan Lipman, "The Border World of Gansu," 249; the battles of 1925 were also described by Mrs. Thomas Moseley, "West China Tidings," *The Alliance Weekly* (February 6, 1926): 87.

167. Mention of the Muslim and Tibetan battle at Labrang in June 1926 by Rev. A.C. Snead, "Crusading for Christ in Far-away Fields: The Kansu-Tibetan Border," *The Alliance Weekly* (August 21, 1926): 544ff.

168. Feng's army was a different force from the Guomindang led by Jiang Jieshi.

169. Detailed in Mrs. Thomas Moseley, "Our Abdullah's Cave: Trophies of Grace in Western China," *The Alliance Weekly* (June 7, 1930): 363.

170. Mrs. M.G. Griebenow [Blanche W. Griebenow], Mrs. C.E. Carlson, and Mrs. C.D. Holton, "Conference in West China," *The Alliance Weekly* (December 19, 1925): 874.

171. *Ibid.*

172. Robert Ekvall, unpublished letter to CMA Headquarters, undated, but written on the occasion of the Griebenows' return to Labrang from their first furlough, October 1928.

173. Robert Carlson, Wheaton, IL, private correspondence to Elaine Griebenow; includes unpublished excerpts of letters from Robert Ekvall, undated.

174. Blanche W. Griebenow, Reminiscences, March 1953. This shows

that in 1927, even after several years in Labrang, the Griebenows were as vulnerable as anyone else.

175. See Elizabeth F. Ekvall, Carol E. Carlson, and Anna Haupberg, "Greetings from the Kansu-Tibetan Border Mission Conference," *The Alliance Weekly* (February 2, 1924): 791ff; for some dates and statistics, see "Tibetan Facts for the Interested," *The Alliance Weekly* (March 8, 1924): 25. See also *The Alliance Weekly*, all numbers in 1923-1928.

176. Carlson, private correspondence to E. Griebenow; for a representative account, see the story of W.E. Simpson (no relation to A.J. Simpson, founder of the CMA), who was murdered while travelling in Kham, written by M.G. Griebenow, "Person to Person Evangelism," *The Alliance Weekly* (May 18, 1946): 312-313.

177. Huang, *Huang*, 26-27.

178. Huang, *rNam thar*, 70.

179. *Chos srid zung 'brel*: the unity of religious and secular authority. See Michael for further discussion.

180. Huang, *rNam thar*, 74.

181. *De la rang dbang tsam nges can du dgos par dmigs pas.* Huang, *rNam thar*, 72.

182. *Ibid.*, 72-73.

183. 1927 marked the beginning of conflict in east China between Chiang Kaishek's Nationalist Party and the emerging Chinese Communist forces.

184. The Hui destroyed Chone Monastery in November 1927.

185. Huang, *Huang*, 43.

186. *Ibid.*, 47.

187. *Ibid.*, 55.

188. *Ibid.*, 44.

189. Huang, *rNam thar*, 105-106.

190. Huang, *Huang*, 55.

191. Huang, *rNam thar*, 106; Huang, *Huang*, 55.

192. "Getting a Foothold on the Tibetan Border," *The Alliance Weekly* (March 15, 1930): 168.

193. A descriptive account of the famine is in E. Torvaldson, "Famine in Our Central China Mission Field" and "Starving Chinese," *The Alliance Weekly* (January 9, 1926): 25ff.

194. See a brief account of the situation of the Salar Muslims in Rev. C.D. Holton, "Among the Salars of the Tibetan Borderland," *The Alliance Weekly* (May 21, 1932): 329ff.

195. Rev. A.J. Fesmire, "Our Foreign Mail Bag," *The Alliance Weekly* (March 22, 1930): 187; see also Rev. A.J. Fesmire, "Through Perils Manifold in Kansuh, West China," *The Alliance Weekly* (December 14, 1929): 809ff.

196. Huang, *Huang*, 47.

197. "How Long, Lord, How Long?: The Moslems of West China Hear the Gospel, and Reject the Savior," *The Alliance Weekly* (May 17, 1930): 315.

198. "Leaves from the Log of a Missionary Yak Caravan," *The Alliance Weekly* (October 10, 1931): 664ff.

199. Huang, *Huang*, 51.

200. *Ibid.*, 61; Huang, *rNam thar*, 150.

201. Huang, *Huang*, 61-65. Among other obstructions to Tibetan unity, Apa Alo notes that even in 1934 there was no auto or engine fuel in Gansu and there was no road from Linxia to Labrang until 1940.

202. Huang, *rNam thar*, 130-131; Huang, *Huang*, 53-54.

203. Apa Alo went on to represent Labrang at a major meeting in 1946, where he met Mao Zedong.

204. The Anti-Japanese War started in 1937. This Eastern Expedition was supposedly against the Japanese, but in fact only attacked the Chinese warlord Yan Xishan.

205. See José I. Cabezón and Roger R. Jackson, eds., *Tibetan Literature: Studies in Genre* (Ithaca: Snow Lion, 1996).

206. Stoddard, 140-145.

207. *Ibid.*, 140.

208. Huang, *Huang*, 32, 42; Huang, *rNam thar*, 76, 99.

209. Huang, *rNam thar*, 77.

210. *Ibid.*, 78-79; especially Huang, *Huang*, 32-33.

211. Huang, *Huang*, 33.

212. Huang, *rNam thar*, 81; two publications cited in Huang, *Huang*, 34.

213. Huang, *Huang*, 36.

214. See Charlene E. Makley, "Gendered Practices and the Inner Sanctum: The Reconstruction of Tibetan Sacred Space in 'China's Tibet,'" *The Tibet Journal* 19/2 (Summer 1994): 63; and others.

215. M.G. Griebenow, "Islam in Tibet," 127-129. This article gives an interesting description of the interactions between Tibetan Muslims and Tibetan Buddhists in the borderlands.

216. The sudden emergence of conflict between long-time neighbors has been described by A.P. Cohen: "Our thesis has been that the symbolic expression of community and its boundaries increases in importance as the actual geo-social boundaries of the community are undermined, blurred or otherwise weakened. Evidence to substantiate this thesis may be found not only in settled communities, but also among those whose members have been dispersed and for whom ritual provides occasions to reconstitute the community. So, to the question, 'why do communities respond assertively to encroachment upon their boundaries?', we can now speculate along the following lines. They do so because their members feel themselves to be under so severe a threat from some extrinsic source that if they do not speak out now they may be silenced for ever. Further, they do so because their members recognize their own voices within them, and because they feel the message of this vocal assemblage, though general, to be informed directly by their own experiences and mentalities. And they do so because their members find their identities as individuals through their occupance of the community's social space: if outsiders trespass in that space, then its occupants' own sense of self is felt to be debased and defaced. This sense is always tenuous when the physical and structural boundaries which previously divided the community from the rest of the world are increasingly blurred. It can therefore easily be depicted as under threat: it is a ready means of mobilizing collectively." Cohen, 50, 109.

BIBLIOGRAPHY

Anderson, Benedict. *Imagined Communities*. London: Verso, 1995.

Aubin, F. "Chinese version of Islam: La version chinoise de l'islam," *Archives Européen de sociologie* 30/2 (1989): 192-220.

Avedon, John. *In Exile from the Land of Snows*. New York: Knopf, 1984.

Beckwith, Christopher I. *The Tibetan Empire in Central Asia*. 4th Edition. Princeton: Princeton University Press, 1993.

Buck, David D. "Introduction." *The Journal of Asian Studies* 53/1 (February 1994): 3-10.

Cabezón, José I. and Roger R. Jackson, eds. *Tibetan Literature: Studies in Genre*. Ithaca: Snow Lion, 1996.

Cao Ruigai, ed. *Labuleng Si*. Beijing: Cultural Publishing House, 1989.

Carlsen, John O. "From the Kansu-Tibetan Border Mission." *The Alliance Weekly*, 12 September 1925, 626-631.

Carlsen, William D. *Tibet: In Search of a Miracle*. New York: Nyack College, 1985.

Carlson, Carol. "Marion Grant Griebenow: His Goal." *The Alliance Witness*, 6 December 1972, 6-7.

Carlson, Robert. Private correspondence to Christian Missionary Alliance Headquarters, undated. CMA Archives, Colorado Springs, CO.

_____. Wheaton, IL. Private correspondence to Elaine Griebenow, undated.

Chang, Hajji Yusuf. "The Hui (Muslim) Minority in China: An Historical Overview." *Journal of the Institute of Muslim Minority Affairs* 8/1 (January 1987): 62-78.

Christie, William. "Christie Letters: May 1891 to October 1907." Unpublished manuscript. Christian Missionary Alliance, Colorado Springs, CO.

_____. "Department of Prayer." *The Alliance Witness*, 27 February 1937, 137.

_____. Unpublished manuscript, 1915.

Cohen, A.P. *The Symbolic Construction of Community*. Chichester: Ellis Horwood, Ltd.; London: Tavistock Publications, 1985.

dKon mchog bstan pa rab rgyas, Brag dgon zhabs drung. *Yul mdo smad kyi ljons su thub bstan rin po che ji ltar dar ba'i tshul gsal bar brjod pa: Deb ther rgya mtsho*. [The Ocean Annals of Amdo]. Reproduced by Lokesh Chandra. Śatapiṭaka Series, 226. New Delhi, 1977.

Dunnell, Ruth W. *The Great State of White and High: Buddhism and State Formation in Eleventh-Century Xia*. Honolulu: University of Hawai'i Press, 1996.

Eckel, Malcolm David. "The Ghost at the Table: On the Study of Buddhism and the Study of Religion." *Journal of the American Academy of Religion* 62/4 (Winter 1994): 1086.

Ekvall, David P. *Outposts or Tibetan Border Sketches*. New York: Alliance Press, 1906.

Ekvall, Elizabeth F., Carol E. Carlson, and Anna Haupberg. "Greetings from the Kansu-Tibetan Border Mission Conference." *The Alliance Weekly*, 2 February 1924, 791ff.

Ekvall, Robert E. "The Opportunity in Northeast Tibet." *The Alliance Weekly*, 27 August 1927, 570ff.

_____. *Cultural Relations on the Kansu-Tibetan Border*. The University of Chicago Press, 1939.

_____. *Gateway to Tibet: The Kansu-Tibetan Border.* Harrisburg: Christian Publications, 1938.

_____. Personal correspondence to Christian Missionary Alliance Headquarters, undated, but written on the occasion of the Griebenows' return to Labrang from their first furlough.

Fairbank, J.K. *China: A New History.* Cambridge: The Belknap Press of Harvard University Press, 1992.

Fairbank, John K., and Albert Feuerwerker. *The Cambridge History of China, Volume 13, Republican China 1912-1949, Part 2.* New York: Cambridge University Press, 1978.

Fesmire, Rev. A.J. "New Openings in Tibet." *The Alliance Weekly,* 5 August 1922.

_____. "Our Foreign Mail Bag." *The Alliance Weekly,* 22 March 1930, 187.

_____. "Through Perils Manifold in Kansuh, West China." *The Alliance Weekly,* 14 December 1929, 809ff.

Fletcher, Joseph. "Ch'ing Inner Asia c. 1800." In *The Cambridge History of China, Volume 10, Late Ch'ing, 1800-1911, Part I,* eds. Denis Twitchett and John K. Fairbank, 35-106. London: Cambridge University Press, 1978.

Forman, Harrison. *Through Forbidden Tibet: An Adventure into the Unknown.* New York: Longmans, Green and Company, 1935.

"Getting a Foothold on the Tibetan Border" *The Alliance Weekly,* 15 March 1930, 168.

Gladney, Dru. "Qingzhen: A Study of Ethnoreligious Identity among Hui Muslim Communities in China." Ph.D. dissertation, University of Washington, Seattle, 1987. Ann Arbor: University Microfilms.

Goldstein, Melvyn C. with Gelek Rimpoche. *A History of Modern Tibet, 1913-1951: The Demise of the Lamaist State.* Berkeley: University of California Press, 1989.

"The Gospel Trumpet Sounding in Labrang, Tibet." *The Alliance Weekly,* 11 June 1932, 376.

Griebenow, Blanche Willars. "A Festival Time in Labrang." *The Alliance Weekly,* 14 October 1939, 649-650.

_____. *The Memoirs of Blanche Griebenow.* Edited by Luke H. Sheng. Unpublished, undated manuscript. Compiled in Brighton, MI, ca. 1988. In the possession of Mei Griebenow.

_____. Reminiscences. Taped March 1953 in Nyack, NY. Transcribed by Mei Griebenow. In the possession of Mei Griebenow.

Griebenow, Blanche Willars, et al. "West China Conference." *The Alliance Weekly,* 13 January 1940, 26.

Griebenow, Blanche Willars, Mrs. C.E. Carlson, and Mrs. C.D. Holton. "Conference in West China." *The Alliance Weekly,* 19 December 1925, 874.

Griebenow, George W. "Recollection of His Life in Tibet." Taped 27 December 1983, in Edina, MN. Transcribed by Mei Griebenow, March 1989. In the possession of Mei Griebenow.

Griebenow, Marion Grant. "Across China in Two Days." *The Alliance Weekly,* 15 February 1941, 104-105.

_____. "A Living Buddha Dies." *The Alliance Weekly,* 21 June 1947, 393.

_____. "Back in Labrang." *The Alliance Weekly,* 18 October 1947, 666.

_____. "God's Miracle of Healing in Tibet." *The Alliance Weekly,* March 1950, 38-44.

_____. "Gospel Triumphs in Tibet." *The Alliance Weekly,* 5 June 1948, 361.

_____. "Islam in Tibet." *The Moslem World* 26. Hartford: Hartford Seminary Foundation, 1936.

_____. "Journey to Sungpan." *The Regions Beyond: Newsletter of the Kansu-Tibetan Border Mission* 2/2 (1941): 10-13.

_____. "Our Foreign Mail Bag." *The Alliance Weekly,* 16 April 1932, 250.

_____. "Our Tibetan Guests." *Kansu-Tibetan Border News* 1/5 (April 1935): 1-3.

_____. "Person to Person Evangelism." *The Alliance Weekly,* 18 May 1946, 312-313.

_____. "Pioneering Up South." *The Alliance Weekly,* 2 March 1940, 136ff.

_____. "Taking Christ to Tibetan Nomads." *The Alliance Weekly*, 1 February 1947, 74-75.

_____. "Tibetan-Border Blessings." *The Alliance Weekly*, 5 August 1922.

_____. "Tibetan Prayer Conference." *The Alliance Weekly*, 25 April 1925, 282.

_____. "Tibetan Religious Festivals." *The Alliance Weekly*, 22 September 1934, 600-601.

_____. "Traveling With a God of Tibet." *The Alliance Weekly*, 14 May 1938, 312-314.

_____. Personal correspondence to Rev. A.C. Snead. March 14, 1949. Currently found in Christian Missionary Alliance Archives, Colorado Springs, CO.

Griebenow, Marion and Blanche, et al. "A Foray Into Tibet: Young Alliance Missionaries in a New Pioneering Venture: Five Hundred Miles on Horseback Through the 'Forbidden Land.'" *The Alliance Weekly*, 12 January 1924.

Gross, Jo-Ann. "Introduction." In *Muslims in Central Asia: Expressions of Identity and Change*, ed. Jo-Ann Gross. Durham and London: Duke University Press, 1992. Pp. 1-23.

Guenther, H.V. "Buddhism in Tibet." In *Buddhism and Asian History*, eds. J.M. Kitagawa and M.D. Cummings. New York: Macmillan, 1989. Pp. 175-187.

Harrison, Robert and Connie. Personal correspondence to Mei Griebenow, January 1992.

Holton, Rev. Carter D. "Among the Salars of the Tibetan Borderland." *The Alliance Weekly*, 21 May 1932, 329ff.

_____. "The Salars of Kansu, West China." *The Alliance Weekly*, 2 September 1933, 552.

"How Long, Lord, How Long?: The Moslems of West China Hear the Gospel, and Reject the Savior." *The Alliance Weekly*, 17 May 1930, 315.

Huang Zhengqing. *Huang Zhengqing Yu Wushi Jiamuyang*. Lanzhou: Gansu People's Publishing Co, 1989.

Huang Zhengqing. *Hvang krin ching blo bzang tshe dbang dang kun mkhyen lnga ba chen po sku mched zung gi rnam thar ba rjes su dran pa zag med ye shes kyi me long (A blo spun mched kyi rnam thar)*. Translated by Klu tshangs rdo phrug. Beijing: People's Publishing House, 1994.

Juergensmeyer, Mark. *Religious Nationalism Confronts the Secular State*. Delhi: The Oxford University Press, 1994. Originally published as *The New Cold War: Religious Nationalism Confronts the Secular State* (Berkeley: University of California Press, 1993).

Karmay, Samten G. "Three Sacred Bon Dances ('Cham)," in Jamyang Norbu, ed. *Zlos-Gar*. Dharamsala: Library of Tibetan Works and Archives, 1986, pp. 58-68.

Kemerer, Lois. Personal correspondence to Mei Griebenow, 8 December 1991.

"Leaves from the Log of a Missionary Yak Caravan." *The Alliance Weekly*, 10 October 1931, 664ff.

Li An Che. *Labrang: A Study in the Field by Li An Che*. Edited by Chie Nakane. Tokyo: Institute of Oriental Culture, The University of Tokyo, 1982. Reprinted as: Li An-che. *History of Tibetan Religion: A Study in the Field*. Beijing: New World Press, 1994.

Lindstrom, Ruth E. "Missionary Mailbag." *Kansu-Tibetan Border News*, 1933, 2.

Lipman, Jonathan N. "The Border World of Gansu, 1895-1935." Ph.D. diss., Stanford University, 1981. Ann Arbor: University Microfilms.

_____. "Ethnicity and Politics in Republican China: The Ma Family Warlords of Gansu." *Modern China* 10/3 (July 1984): 285-316.

_____. "Ethnic Violence in Modern China: Hans and Hui in Gansu, 1781-1929." In *Violence in China: Essays in Culture and Counterculture*, ed. Jonathan N. Lipman and Steven Harrell. Albany: State University of New York Press, 1990. Pp. 65-88.

Luo Faxi, ed. *Labuleng Si Gai Kuang*. Lanzhou: People's Publishing House, 1990.

Makley, Charlene E. "Gendered Practices and the Inner Sanctum: The Reconstruction of Tibetan Sacred Space in 'China's Tibet.'" *The Tibet Journal* 19/2 (Summer 1994): 63.

McCormack, Gavan. *Chang Tso-lin in Northeast China, 1911-1928: China, Japan, and the Manchurian Idea*. Stanford: Stanford University Press, 1977.

Michael, Franz. *Rule by Incarnation: Tibetan Buddhism and Its Role in Society and State*. Boulder: Westview Press, 1982.

Moseley, Rev. Thomas. "Back to the Kansu-Tibetan Border." *The Alliance Weekly*, 20 June 1931, 401.

_____. "A Night in a Tibetan Nomad Tent." *The Alliance Weekly*, 2 December 1933, 760.

Moseley, Mrs. M. "Our Abdullah's Cave: Trophies of Grace in Western China." *The Alliance Weekly*, 7 June 1930, 363.

Moseley, Mrs. Thomas. "West China Tidings." *The Alliance Weekly*, 6 February 1926, 87.

Naquin, Susan and Chun-fang Yu, eds. *Pilgrims and Sacred Sites in China*. Berkeley: University of California Press, 1992.

Norbu, Jamyang with Tashi Dhondup. "A Preliminary Study of Gar, The Court Dance and Music of Tibet," in Jamyang Norbu, ed. *Zlos-Gar*. Dharamsala: Library of Tibetan Works and Archives, 1986, pp. 132-142.

Palbar, Tenzin. *Nga'i pha yul gyi ya nga ba'i lo rgyus*. [The Tragedy of My Homeland]. Dharamsala: Narthang Publications, 1994.

Pan, Yihong. "Sino-Tibetan Treaties in the Tang Dynasty." *T'oung Pao* 78 (1992): 116-161.

Petech, L. *China and Tibet in the Early XVIIIth Century: History of the Establishment of Chinese Protectorate in Tibet*. Leiden: E.J. Brill, 1972.

Pillsbury, Barbara L.K. "Pig and Policy: Maintenance of Boundaries Between Han and Muslim Chinese," *Ethnic Groups* 1/2 (1976): 151-162.

Ray, Reginald A. *Buddhist Saints in India: A Study in Buddhist Values and Orientations*. New York: Oxford University Press, 1994.

Rijnhart, Susie Carlson. *With the Tibetans in Tent and Temple*. Chicago: Fleming H. Revell Company, 1901.

Rockhill, William Woodville. *The Land of the Lamas*. New York: The Century Company, 1891.

Rogers, John D. "Post-Orientalism and the Interpretation of Premodern and Modern Political Identities: The Case of Śri Laṅkā." *The Journal of Asian Studies* 53/1 (February 1994): 10-23.

Ruegg, D. Seyfort. "*mchod yon, yon mchod* and *mchod gnas/yon gnas*: On the Historiography and Semantics of a Tibetan Religio-Social and Religio-Political Concept," in *Tibetan History and Language: Studies Dedicated to Uray Geza on His Seventieth Birthday*, ed. Ernst Steinkellner. Wien, Austria: Arbeitskreis für Tibetische und Buddhistische Studien, 1991. Pp. 441-454.

_____. "Vajrayāna Buddhism in the Western Himālaya." *Acta Indologica* VI, 1984.

Shabdrung Tshang, Alak. *Thub bstan yongs su rdzogs pa'i mnga' bdag kun gzigs ye shes kyi nyi ma chen po 'jam dbyangs bzhad pa'i rdo rje 'pheng lnga'i rnam par thar ba mdor bsdus su bkod pa* [The Fifth Jamyang Shaypa, 1916-1947]. Nanjing, 1948. Archive copy, Library of Tibetan Works and Archives, Dharamsala, India.

Sheridan, James E. *China in Disintegration: The Republican Era in Chinese History, 1912-1949*. New York: The Free Press, 1975.

Snead, Rev. A.C. "Crusading for Christ in Far-away Fields: The Kansu-Tibetan Border." *The Alliance Weekly*, 21 August 1926, 544ff.

Stubel, Hans. *The Mewu Fantzu: A Tibetan Tribe of Kansu*. New Haven: Hraf Press, 1958.

Stoddard, Heather. *Le Mendiant de l'Amdo*. Paris: Société d'Ethnographie, 1986.

Tambiah, Stanley. *The Buddhists Saints of the Forest and the Cult of Amulets*. New York: Cambridge University Press, 1984.

Teichman, Eric. *Travels of a Consular Officer in Eastern Tibet*. Cambridge University Press, 1922.

"Tibetan Facts for the Interested." *The Alliance Weekly*, 8 March 1924, 25.

Torvaldson, E. "Famine in Our Central China Mission Field." *The Alliance Weekly*, 9 January 1926, 25ff.

_____. "Starving Chinese." *The Alliance Weekly*, 9 January 1926, 25ff.

Von Erffa, Wolfgang. *Uncompromising Tibet: Tradition-Religion-Politics.* English Revised Edition. New Delhi: Paljor Publications, 1996. First published in German by Edition Interfrom, Zurich, 1992.

White, Richard. *The Middle Ground: Indians, Empires, and the Republics in the Great Lakes Region, 1650-1815.* New York: Cambridge University Press, 1991.

Yang, Ho-chin. *The Annals of Kokonor.* Bloomington: Indiana University, 1969.

Yon tan rgya mtsho [Yontan Gyatso]. *Chos sde chen po bla brang bkra shis 'khyil: mkhas grub 'bum sde'i rol mtsho mdo sngags bstan pa'i 'byung gnas dga' ldan bshad sgrub bkra shis 'khyil gyi skor bzhad gzhung dal 'bab mdzod yangs las nye bar sgrub pa sngon med legs bshad ngo mtshar bkra shis chos dung bzhad pa'i sgra dbyangs.* Paris: n.p., 1987.

Zwemer, Dr. Samuel M. "On the Frontiers of Northwest China." *The Alliance Weekly,* 28 October 1933, 680ff.

INDEX